The Experts' Book of
Crossword Puzzle Making

The Experts' Book of Crossword Puzzle Making

VERA DANIELS

Doubleday & Company, Inc., Garden City, New York   1976

Library of Congress Cataloging in Publication Data

Daniels, Vera.
The experts' book of crossword puzzle making.

1. Crossword puzzles.   I.   Title.
GV1507.C7D325   793.73′2
ISBN 0-385-02173-9
Library of Congress Catalog Card Number 74–18843

Contents

The Experts' Book of
Crossword Puzzle Making

1 Getting Started

Are you interested in earning extra money in your spare time? Are you having trouble finding a profitable hobby? Why not try crossword puzzle constructing?

Crossword puzzles are fascinating, profitable, and easy to construct.

No previous experience or special writing ability is required. If you can read, write, and draw a straight line with the aid of a ruler, you have the ability to construct salable crossword puzzles.

Editors of crossword puzzle magazines purchase thousands of different types of word puzzles each month. They pay the contributors from $3.00 to $10 per puzzle—depending, of course, on the size and type of puzzle.

It generally comes as a surprise to most people to learn that editors of crossword puzzle magazines often purchase as many as three hundred or four hundred new word puzzles each month from crossword puzzle contributors. The fact is that practically all publishers of crossword puzzle magazines publish four or five different crossword puzzle magazines each month. In fact, some publishers publish as many as seven and eight puzzle periodicals each month. Each crossword puzzle magazine contains on an average of seventy-five word puzzles. Some magazines are made up exclusively of crossword puzzles; others are made up of a variety of different types of word puzzles.

If you can supply editors of crossword puzzle magazines with the kind of puzzles they need, they will buy from you even if you have never before submitted a crossword puzzle for publication. Crossword puzzle constructing is one field that isn't overcrowded because the opportunities in this field aren't publicized.

The time you devote to crossword puzzle constructing may range from a full-day schedule to a part-time hobby, or just an occasional try at breaking into print with a crossword puzzle.

And remember, too, there is plenty of room in this field for your puzzles. New crossword puzzle magazines are entering this field, and the old stand-bys are getting bigger and better. More puzzles are needed, and you can fill a part of this huge demand. It all makes sense, doesn't it? So don't put it off any longer. Get started in this field, and receive your share of these monthly checks.

This entire course is based, designed, and compiled from practical experience—trial and error. It contains many practical hints, do's, don'ts, as well as a set of established rules and guidelines that you must follow if you want to construct interesting puzzles that sell.

Successful puzzle constructors depend primarily on the knowledge of rules and guidelines. Thus, the beginner who usually succeeds in this field is the one who learns these rules and guidelines and follows them precisely to the letter.

All the basic elements and other important subject matter pertinent to the construction of salable crossword puzzles have been carefully evaluated, compiled, and presented in simple terms to make it possible for the beginner to follow the instructions easily and expertly. The arrangement and the grouping of topics is presented in a series of steps that produce the most successful results in the most practical way and in the shortest time.

At first, if the arrangement of the chapters in this book confuses you, don't worry. When you read the entire book and clearly understand the basic principles of crossword puzzle construction, you will find that all the chapters in this book fit together nicely to form a complete unit.

In addition to the instruction for constructing regular crossword puzzles, you will also find complete instructions for constructing a variety of other types of word puzzles for which there also is a great demand. The other types of word puzzles are:

The topical crossword puzzle

The diagramless crossword puzzle
The make-it-yourself crossword puzzle
The fill-in crossword puzzle
The acrostic puzzle
The progressive blocks puzzle
The chain word puzzle
The overlap word puzzle

Please keep in mind the fact that the instructions in the first 21 chapters of this book deal primarily with the regular crossword puzzle. This puzzle is the basic puzzle from which all other types of word puzzles originated. Therefore, it's important that the beginner learn to construct the regular crossword puzzle before making an attempt to construct other types of word puzzles. Full knowledge of the "regular crossword puzzle" will simplify the construction of other types of word puzzles.

In order to get the full benefit from the instructions in this book, I recommend that the beginner read the entire contents of this book several times.

First, read the entire book to get an over-all picture of all the different types of word puzzles that are used by most crossword puzzle magazines.

In the second reading, take plenty of time and study the individual instructions thoroughly so that you understand them clearly. If you don't understand any specific part of the instructions clearly, go over them until they are thoroughly and clearly understood. In time you will discover that you can construct many different types of word puzzles without referring to the instructions in the book. It may be a good idea, however, to keep this book handy just in case you're not absolutely clear on any specific subject.

So . . . get your material together, read the instructions carefully and start constructing crossword puzzles. Start slowly if you must, but get started, and good luck.

TOOLS OF THE TRADE

You must have good tools to do good work. This is an important rule, so don't disregard it.

In crossword puzzle constructing—as in any other profession— there are certain tools of the trade that are essential in the production of high-quality work—work that has that professional look and can be produced only by master mechanics.

To be fully equipped for constructing crossword puzzles (or any other type of word puzzles) you will need the following articles:

1 typewriter
1 dictionary
1 12″ ruler (metal edge)
1 fountain pen
1 bottle of black India ink
1 small pointed artist's brush
Supply of typewriter paper
Supply of envelopes and stamps
1 postal scale (optional)

The typewriter is one of the most essential and useful tools in the construction of crossword puzzles. Any attempt to construct crossword puzzles without one is sheer folly. In order to draw accurately spaced diagrams and to produce neat, professional-looking puzzles of a high caliber, you must use a typewriter.

Typewriters are manufactured in different models, and they come equipped with a variety of type styles and sizes. The elite-type size, which is the smaller of the two sizes, produces nice-looking copies; it is generally used for business correspondence. The pica-type size, which is most generally used by writers, is larger than the elite. The reason most writers use this type size is that it produces manuscripts that are easy to read.

However, for the construction of crossword puzzles (or any other type of word puzzles) you can use either elite or the pica type, and your puzzles will be accepted by the editors. Personally, for the construction of crossword puzzles, I prefer the elite type.

If you would like to construct puzzles but you don't own a typewriter, perhaps you can borrow one from a friend or a relative until you can purchase one of your own. Or, perhaps, you can rent one by the month from a typewriter dealer. I suggest, however, that you purchase a used typewriter instead of renting one by the month; you will find it to be much cheaper in the long run. There are many used typewriters on the market that are in good working condition, and they can be purchased cheaply on monthly installments.

If there aren't any used typewriter dealers in your town or in your community, insert a small ad in the "Wanted" section of your local newspaper. Usually a small ad will bring good results. It's really surprising how many good typewriters are collecting dust in someone's attic or closet. If you decide to purchase a used typewriter, don't worry too much about the age, the model, or the make of the typewriter, just as long as the price is reasonable and it works properly to produce clear legible copies. If you produce puzzles of a high caliber, the editors won't know whether your puzzles were produced on an old, used typewriter or on a new, expensive one, and they will probably care less.

Another important accessory that is essential in the art of crossword puzzle construction is a good, reliable dictionary.

Whenever you submit crossword puzzles (or any other type of word puzzles) to an editor for his consideration, you must also include the name of the dictionary from which the words and the definitions for your puzzles were taken.

Some editors merely request—without being specific—that the source of reference (the name of the dictionary which you use in the construction of your puzzles) be included in the general information that is usually printed in the upper right-hand corner of the diagram page. There are some editors, however, who specifically name the dictionaries in which the words and the definitions in your puzzles must be found.

If you don't have a dictionary at the present time but intend to purchase one, I suggest that you select a dictionary you can depend on. One of the most reliable sources of information for your crossword puzzles is Webster's New Collegiate Dictionary. It is an ideal dictionary for the beginner in the field of crossword puzzle construction. Besides being reliable and inexpensive, this dictionary is accepted as an authoritative source of reference by practically all editors of crossword puzzle magazines. It contains 130,000 entries. In addition to the many foreign words, synonyms, prefixes, suffixes, combining form words, and the correct spelling of plurals in the general vocabulary section, the dictionary also contains 5,000 names of noted people with dates, nationality, and status or occupation in the Biographical Section. The Pronouncing Gazetteer contains 12,000 geographical names throughout the world—countries, cities, towns, rivers, lakes, mountains, etc. In addition, it contains hundreds of common English given names, and 3,700 common abbreviations.

Purchase a 12-inch ruler with a metal edge and a cheap cartridge pen (use permanent black-ink cartridges). These two articles are used for drawing diagrams.

You'll also need a good grade of black waterproof India ink to fill in the unused squares in the diagrams. I recommend that you purchase Carter's brand India ink for this purpose; it produces deep, rich, black squares. Be sure to shake the ink well before you use it. Otherwise, your black squares may turn out to be a muddy brown.

You will need a small pointed artist's brush to ink in the unused squares in the diagrams. I recommend a ⚞3 pointed sable brush for this purpose. A sable brush is somewhat more expensive than a camel hair brush, but you will find it much easier to work with the sable. In addition, a sable brush will hold up better and outlast a camel hair brush. When you are through using the brush, wash it with soap in lukewarm water to remove the excess ink. Shape the hair to a point before you put it away to dry.

For all types of puzzles, use standard 8½×11 white bond paper (20 lb. weight). It's cheaper when you purchase it by the ream (500 sheets).

Purchase an adequate supply of ⚞10, ⚞11, and 9×12 envelopes and postage stamps.

When you submit only one or two puzzles to an editor, you may mail them in a ⚞11 envelope. Use the ⚞10 envelope as a stamped self-addressed envelope. It fits nicely into a ⚞11 envelope. However, I prefer to submit them—particularly when I'm submitting more than two puzzles at one time—in a 9×12 envelope. The large envelope permits you to mail your puzzles flat—without any folds or creases. All editors prefer to have the puzzles that are submitted for their consideration to be mailed flat in large envelopes. Puzzles submitted in this manner are more convenient to handle and easier to read than puzzles that have been folded to fit the smaller size envelopes.

Another good reason why you should submit your puzzles in large envelopes is that if your puzzles aren't accepted for publication, they will be returned in their original condition—flat, unfolded, and ready to be resubmitted to a different publisher.

All typed material—and that includes crossword puzzles—must be sent as first class mail.

And remember, too, whenever you submit any kind of puzzles to an editor, it's customary that your puzzles be accompanied by a self-addressed envelope with a sufficient amount of postage attached to the envelope for the return of your puzzles if they aren't accepted for publication. Otherwise, an editor is under no obligation to return your puzzles.

Whenever I submit a batch of puzzles to an editor, I always paper clip a sufficient amount of postage to a 9×12 self-addressed envelope which I fold in two. If an editor decides to accept my puzzles for publication, the stamps will not be wasted. The editor can make use of them in any way he sees fit. After all, I feel that it's a small price to pay for having my puzzles accepted for publication. On the other hand, if the puzzles are rejected, I will still be out the same amount of postage.

It isn't necessary to own a postal scale. There is, however, a definite advantage to be gained by having one and using it to weigh your puzzles. If you own a postal scale, you can weigh the envelope that contains your puzzles in your own home, affix the correct amount of postage to the envelope, and drop it into the nearest mail box—any time of the day or night, including Sundays and holidays.

On the other hand, if you don't own a postal scale, you can either take a guess at the correct amount of postage required to send your puzzles through the mail, or you must take your puzzles to a post office and have them weighed by a postal clerk. Frequent trips to a post office, besides being inconvenient, can also be costly and time-consuming, especially if the post office is a great distance away from your home and you must use a car or some other means of transportation to reach it.

You must also take into consideration the possibility of bad weather, and the fact that you can visit the post office only during the hours when it is open for business—which, unfortunately, happens to coincide with the working hours of most people.

THE REQUIREMENT SHEET

The requirement sheet for crossword puzzles, which can be had on request from editors of crossword puzzle magazines, contains a set of rules and guidelines that you must follow to the letter if you wish to sell your puzzles.

Besides setting up specific rules and guidelines to follow, the requirement sheet will give you valuable information on the following subjects:

Sizes and types of puzzles that are used by the magazine.
Kind of words to use in the diagram.
Kind of words to avoid in the diagram.

Style and setup.
How to draw the diagram page.
How to prepare the definition pages.
The mechanical requirements.
Criteria.
Rates.
How to submit puzzles.

In addition, the requirement sheet will usually give you other bits of valuable information with reference to the crossword puzzle.

Each editor seems to have his or her own specific requirements for crossword puzzles and other types of word puzzles.

The requirements for crossword puzzles vary from publication to publication. So if you decide to submit a few puzzles to a specific publication, write to the editor and tell him or her that you would like to submit a few crossword puzzles for his consideration, and that you would like to have his requirement sheet for crossword puzzles. Be sure to enclose a large, stamped, self-addressed envelope with your request.

If you would like to submit other types of word puzzles, such as acrostic, fill-in puzzles, etc., write to the editor and ask for requirement sheets for these particular types of puzzles. Generally, most editors have requirements sheets for all types of word puzzles published in their magazines.

In order to save yourself valuable time and money—for paper, envelopes, postage, etc.—don't attempt to submit any type of word puzzle to an editor unless you are thoroughly familiar with the editor's requirements.

In addition to studying the editor's requirement sheets, I strongly suggest that you also study several current issues of the crossword puzzle magazines that are put out by the publisher to whom you intend to submit your puzzles. This will not only give you a general idea of the types and sizes of puzzles used by the publisher, but it will also give you an excellent idea of the different styles and setups that the magazines use.

The thing that I want to emphasize is that if you want to sell puzzles to the editors of puzzle magazines, you must follow the rules and guidelines as set forth in the requirement sheets. This is advice from one who knows. If you ignore it, then you're wasting your time constructing puzzles that will never sell.

Sometimes editors may break a few of their own rules, but that is their privilege. Editors can do practically anything they please. But remember, you're no editor. Regardless of how trivial or unimportant some of the instructions may appear to you, carry them out to the letter; don't break any rules.

Whatever *you* think isn't important; it's what the editors think and demand that is really important. After all, *they're* the ones who purchase the puzzles and mail out the checks. So, follow their instructions to the letter, and you will become a successful puzzle constructor.

WORDS TO BE AVOIDED

You should try to construct crossword puzzles that are interesting to solve. Without being trite, use words that are found in the ordinary dictionary—words that are used in everyday conversation.

Some requirement sheets give a complete list of the kind of words that should be avoided in all types of word puzzles, and some say nothing—not one single word—about the kind of words that should or should not be used in word puzzles.

However, from my own personal experience and observation, in addition to studying various requirement sheets, I will attempt to give you a general rundown on the kind of words that you should avoid in your puzzles.

Avoid, if you possibly can, hackneyed words that appear frequently in poor crossword puzzles.

Avoid, if you possibly can, archaic (arch.), obsolete (obs.), dialect (dial.), slang (sl.), colloquial (colloq., coll.), variants (var.), foreign words (Fr., Ger., Sp., etc.), and mythological terms—especially in easy and medium puzzles.

Avoid, if you possibly can, names of persons, cities, rivers, mountains, etc. not familiar to most people and strange words that are not used in everyday conversation; they are considered to be difficult words and should be avoided in puzzles.

Avoid the use of phrases in a given space in the diagram.

Even though many editors permit the use of two or more words in a given space in the diagram, I still make it a rule to use only single words in all my crossword puzzle diagrams because I find that I can construct interesting and salable puzzles by using only single words in the diagrams. The advantage of using only single words is that if my puzzles are rejected by one editor, I can always resubmit them to another editor—even to an editor who doesn't permit the practice of using two or more words in a given space in the diagrams.

When you construct crossword puzzles, I suggest that you construct them in a manner that will permit you to submit them, without fear, to any editor in the business. Sometimes, if a puzzle is rejected, you may have to retype the definition pages to conform to the format of the next magazine to which you intend to submit the puzzle. However, retyping the definitions is a minor problem.

And by all means, avoid the use of words—even short ones—that require long or complicated definitions. Make it a rule to check every unfamiliar word before you enter it in the diagram. Reject any word that requires a detailed definition, and substitute for it an easier word that carries a simpler definition. I must admit, however, that there will be many occasions when you will not be able to find a substitute word with an easier definition. I don't mean that you can't use a controversial word (or words) in your puzzle diagrams. Use them if you can or must, as long as the editors tolerate and accept them. In fact, many times controversial words can help to get you out of a tight spot or even solve a minor problem, and allow you to complete your puzzles quickly. I can assure you, however, that your puzzles will be more interesting, and they will stand a better chance of being accepted for publication if you simply omit controversial words.

The best advice that I can offer you on this subject is that you must be guided by the publisher's requirement sheet and his crossword puzzle magazines. Some editors accept certain words (sometimes reluctantly), and some editors reject them entirely. So before you use a controversial word in any of your puzzles, be absolutely sure that the editors to whom you intend to submit your puzzles accept them.

Experience is really the best teacher. After you have been in this business—if you care to call it that—for any length of time, you soon learn to select your words wisely. You learn, quickly, which words you can safely use in your puzzles, and which words you must avoid.

Some editors, in fact, will even help you (unintentionally, of course) to compile a list of words to be avoided. Many times when an editor rejects a puzzle he will make some sort of comment about it and mark off certain words in the diagram that he doesn't approve of.

Restrict the excessive use of abbreviations (abbrs.) in crossword puzzle diagrams—use them only as a last resort. Some editors limit the number of abbreviations they permit in a specific size puzzle, and some editors set no limit on them. Whenever editors refer to abbreviations in crossword puzzles, they usually refer to the actual abbreviations you use in the diagram section of the puzzle and not to the definition pages.

Abbreviations, such as Fr., Ger., Sp., pref., suff., etc., that are usually found in the definitions are not counted as abbreviations.

Examples:

1. Beach (Fr.)   PLAGE
2. High (Scot.)   BRENT
3. Mister (Ger.)   HERR
4. Before (pref.)   RE

But whenever you use the actual abbreviation form in the definition, then you must count it as an abbreviation in the puzzle.

Examples:

1. East-southeast (abbr.)   ESE
2. German (abbr.)   GER
3. Alabama (abbr.)   ALA
4. Prefix (abbr.)   PREF

If an editor doesn't specifically state in his requirement sheet the number of abbreviations that he permits in the puzzle diagrams of different sizes, then I firmly recommend that you study several recent issues of that editor's crossword puzzle magazines. Count the number of abbreviations in the different sizes of puzzles in the magazines, and you will usually get a fairly accurate idea of the number of abbreviations allowed by that particular magazine.

As an additional bit of information, I would like to point out that whenever you fail to find a suitable abbreviation for a designated space in the diagram, you can usually substitute an abbreviation with a prefix, suffix, chemical symbol, combining form word or a Roman numeral. (Whenever a Roman numeral that contains the figure 1 is used in a diagram, the number "1" represents the letter "i." For example, the Roman numeral for 7 reads as "v" double "i"; thus, "vii." LI for 50 reads as "li," and II for 2 reads as "ii," etc.)

I make it a rule—which I break occasionally, if I am permitted—to limit the number of abbreviations in my puzzles as follows: one abbreviation in an 11×11 or 13×13 size puzzle; two in a 15×15; three in a 17×17 and 19×19; four in a 21×21; and five in a

23×23. These are my own rules, and you don't have to follow them. Use your own judgment as to how many abbreviations you want to use in a specific size puzzle.

During my time as a crossword puzzle constructor, I have examined and studied many, many different crossword puzzle magazines. I have found that in some puzzle magazines, abbreviations (in the diagrams) were rather scarce, even in some of the large size puzzles, while in other puzzle magazines, abbreviations were quite numerous —even in the smaller size puzzles. On the whole, however, the great majority of the puzzles contained either one or two abbreviations or none at all.

Crossword puzzles—large or small—that contain a minimum number of abbreviations in the diagrams stand a much better chance of being accepted for publication than puzzles that contain a large number of abbreviations. (Personally, I fail to see why some editors are so fussy about the number of abbreviations that may be used in a single crossword puzzle. Two abbreviations. Four abbreviations. What's the difference? I usually find it much easier to find an abbreviation for a specific definition than I do to find a word for a difficult definition. However, like all other puzzle constructors, I, too, must abide by the editors' rules if I want to continue to sell to them.)

Make up three individual lists of two-, three- and four-letter abbreviations, prefixes, suffixes, chemical symbols, combining form words, and the basic Roman numerals. Keep these three lists of abbreviations handy whenever you work on puzzles. You will be amazed at how much valuable time you can save when you want to find a suitable abbreviation—or a specific combination of letters—to fit into a designated space in the diagram. You will find that you will not have to search through the entire dictionary for them. You will find what you need easily and quickly in your lists. (Later you can add these lists of abbreviations to your classified lists of words if you decide to compile them.)

Restrict the use of two- and three-letter words in the diagram sections of your puzzles; they make the puzzles uninteresting. In fact, some editors limit the number of two- and three-letter words in a single puzzle; keep them at a minimum.

Never use the same word (or another form of the same word) in the same puzzle diagram. Examples: sing, sang, sung, singing; walk, walked, walker, walking; eat, ate, eaten, eater, eating, etc.

Never use hyphenated words in the puzzle diagram. Examples:

self-help, self-starter, re-enact, etc.

Never use trade-marks or trade names in any section of the puzzle.

Under no condition use anatomical, physiological, or similar words; names of diseases or words pertaining to death or sickness. Morbid words such as behead, bier, coffin, cemetery, crippled, death, dirge, execute, funeral, gallows, graveyard, hearse, insane, ill, imbecile, invalid, infirm, kill, lame, morbid, moron, mortuary, obit, plague, slaughter, sick, tomb, unhealthy, etc. are considered to be "offensive words"; they don't belong in crossword puzzles. Many puzzle fans are invalids; they aren't interested in morbid, unpleasant or offensive words. So choose your words accordingly; otherwise, many of your puzzles may be rejected.

Occasionally, you may find a few offensive words in some crossword puzzles. The reason for this, I suppose, is that there are a few editors who don't consider them to be taboo. However, if you really want to become a popular crossword puzzle contributor with the editors of puzzle magazines, I strongly recommend that you never—and I mean never—use any morbid, offensive, or unpleasant words in any of your puzzles. Puzzles should be constructed for fun and pleasure. Use happy words.

THE VOCABULARY

The vocabulary is simply a stock of words used in speaking and writing.

People aren't born with vocabularies. They acquire them gradually over a period of time.

Some people seem to acquire a large vocabulary without any difficulty. For others, regardless of how vigorously they try, it's a task.

Obviously, words are the functional tools of crossword puzzle constructors. In fact, they are the basic elements for all types of word puzzles. It will pay you to study them well and become thoroughly familiar with the many ways they are used in word puzzles.

The crossword puzzle constructor (beginner or professional) with a large vocabulary will find it much easier to find suitable words for his puzzles than the puzzle constructor who has a limited vocabulary. However, to become a successful crossword puzzle constructor, it really isn't necessary to have a large vocabulary at the tip of your tongue. Just keep a reliable dictionary handy, use it frequently, and you, too, can construct salable puzzles.

If you are an avid crossword puzzle fan, you probably are familiar with many strange words that are found in today's puzzles—words which, perhaps, you never knew existed.

In most of today's crossword puzzles you can find many foreign words; slang words and expressions; obsolete, archaic and colloquial words; many strange phrases, scientific terminology, mythological names and places.

Unless you are an avid crossword puzzle fan, you will not know that *roi* means king in French; *dit* means poem in French; *das, des,* and *ein* means article in German; *mime* means drama in Greek; *leste* means Madeira wind, and *pasta* means dough in Italian, just to mention a few.

Incidentally, at this point, a word of warning to the beginner is in order. Regardless of how many difficult, strange, or foreign words you are familiar with, never—and I mean never—use them in your puzzle diagrams unless the specific word (or words) is actually found in the dictionary that you use and name as a source of reference.

If an editor or a checker can't find a specific word from your puzzle diagram in the dictionary that you name as a source of reference, your puzzle will be automatically rejected—even if your puzzle is constructed perfectly in all other respects.

Each word in the diagram section of the puzzle must be verified. Editors will not accept any word—particularly a word that is unfamiliar to them—without checking it out first. In fact, some editors will not accept many foreign words that they don't like even if they can be found in the dictionary.

If you're a beginner in the crossword puzzle field and have a limited vocabulary, don't let it worry you, because there are several methods that you can use to increase the range of your present vocabulary.

First of all, I would like to point out that the following information isn't intended to be a vocabulary booster or a lesson in grammar.

The following information will merely point out several simple methods you can apply, in crossword puzzle constructing, to increase the length of many short, basic words by one, two, or three letters—stretch them, so to speak—so that many short words can be extended to fill in longer spaces in the diagrams. You can do this by merely following a few simple rules of grammar—rules with which you are most likely familiar. However, just in case you've forgotten any of these rules, perhaps a few simple examples may help to refresh your memory.

The first method that you can use to increase the length of many nouns is very simple to follow: the use of plurals.

(Incidentally, nouns are the only words you can change from a singular form to a plural; some adjectives such as reds, blues, greens, etc., when they are used as nouns, may also be used in the plural forms.)

In this first example, you can add the letter "s" to singular nouns to form plurals; this simple addition increases the length of many nouns by one extra letter. Examples: car, cars; war, wars; camel, camels; wagon, wagons; garden, gardens; apartment, apartments; etc.

In this second example, you can add the letters "es" to many singular nouns to form plurals; thus, increasing the length of many nouns by two extra letters. Examples: dish, dishes; wish, wishes; miss, misses; veto, vetoes; potato, potatoes; radish, radishes; etc.

In singular nouns that end with the letter "y" after any letter except a, e, i, o, or u, change the "y" to "i" and add "es." Examples: fly, flies; sty, sties; spy, spies; copy, copies; etc.

There's a group of singular nouns that end with the letters "f," "fe," or "ff." To change them to plurals, add the letter "s." Examples: scarf, scarfs; safe, safes, staff, staffs; etc.

However, in some nouns of this group that end with the letters "f" or "fe," change the "f" or "fe" to "v" and add "es." Examples: calf, calves; wife, wives; thief, thieves; beef, beeves; leaf, leaves; loaf, loaves; etc.

Certain nouns in the singular form can be changed to a plural by adding either an "s" or an "es" to the singular form nouns.

Examples:

singular	plural	plural
buffalo	buffalos	buffaloes
banjo	banjos	banjoes
cargo	cargos	cargoes
flamingo	flamingos	flamingoes

There are many nouns in the English language that change their forms considerably when they are changed from a singular form to a plural. Examples: ox, oxen; foot, feet; child, children; mouse, mice; goose, geese; genus, genera; etc.

And to avoid unlikely plurals in your puzzle diagrams, you should become familiar with many nouns that are identical in both the singular and the plural form.

Examples:

singular	*plural*	*singular*	*plural*
Bantu	Bantu	moose	moose
deer	deer	Siamese	Siamese
elk	elk	swine	swine
grouse	grouse	Iroquois	Iroquois

Also, keep in mind the fact that abbreviations, as well as complete words, can be changed from a singular form to a plural. Examples: lb., lbs.; oz., ozs.; sta., stas.; dep., deps.; etc.

And here is another word of caution to the beginner. Whenever you use plural words in the diagram sections of your crossword puzzles, be absolutely sure that they are spelled correctly. In fact, if there is any doubt about the correct spelling of any words (singular or plural), look the words up in your dictionary for their correct spelling.

A crossword puzzle (or any other type of word puzzle) that contains a misspelled word in the diagram section will be rejected automatically by an editor, because it's practically impossible to correct a misspelled word in the diagram without changing many of the adjoining and crossing words.

Some editors may take the time to correct a misspelled word or two in the "definition section" of your puzzle, or they may even go so far as to change an entire definition that they don't like. But they cannot be expected to take the time or the trouble to correct a misspelled word in the diagram section of your puzzle. The best advice that I can offer on this particular subject is: If you're not absolutely sure of the correct spelling of any word in your puzzle (either in the diagram or the definition section), don't guess at it; look the word up in your dictionary. This simple precaution may prevent many of your puzzles from being rejected.

The second method, which you can use to increase the length of many verbs by one, two, or three extra letters, is also quite simple to follow.

In this method, you merely change the tenses of the verbs from the present tense to the past tense. Examples: lie, lied; tie, tied; copy, copied; cook, cooked; tar, tarred; slip, slipped; scar, scarred; etc.

Or you can use the present tense forms of many verbs and still increase their length by one, two, or three extra letters. Examples: give, gives, giving; look, looks, looking; stare, stares, staring; start, starts, starting; walk, walks, walking; rip, rips, ripping; etc.

The third method, which you can use to add two, three, and sometimes four extra letters to many adjectives (or adverbs, depending, of course, on how you use them), is to simply apply the three degrees of comparison to them as shown in the following examples:

rich	richer	richest
big	bigger	biggest
thin	thinner	thinnest
clean	cleaner	cleanest
smooth	smoother	smoothest
slow	slower	slowest
fast	faster	fastest

The fourth method, which you can use to increase the length of many verbs, adverbs, and adjectives, is also quite simple to follow.

In this method, you can make use of prefixes and suffixes—that is, you can add a prefix or a suffix to a root word.

The most popular and practical prefix, which is used most frequently in crossword puzzle diagrams by practically all puzzle constructors in the business, is the prefix "re." It means (1) back, (2) again.

Keep this particular prefix in mind at all times when you work on the diagram sections of your puzzles; it can help you out of many tight spots. You can add this particular prefix to a multitude of verbs. In fact, you can even form and use many words—in the diagram sections of your puzzles—that can't be found in your dictionary. However, they will be accepted as legitimate words by the editors of crossword puzzle magazines. Examples: rewalk, resang, resew, reseed, rebow, rebend, reran, rerun, recap, redip, retar, rehunt, recamp, recool, etc.

And while I am still on the subject of words, I would like to point out the additional advantage of using one of the better dictionaries as your source of reference.

Generally, cheap dictionaries, which can be purchased for one or two dollars, contain only the basic words in the general vocabulary; even many of the common words are missing from the cheap dictionaries. On the other hand, the better dictionaries, which can be purchased for as little as six or seven dollars, contain not only the basic words in the general vocabulary but also many other forms of the same words, as shown in a few of the following examples:

can	canned, canner, canning.
cool	cooler, coolish, cooly, coolness.
dim	dimmer, dimmest, dimmed, dimming, dimly, dimness.
flavor	flavored, flavorer, flavorless, flavorous.
large	larger, largest, largely, largeness.
slim	slimmed, slimmer, slimmest, slimming, slimly, slimness.
slope	sloped, sloping, sloper, slopingly.
smell	smelled or smelt, smelling, smellable, smeller.
thin	thinner, thinnest, thinned, thinning, thinly, thinness.

HOW TO COMPILE CLASSIFIED WORD LISTS

The classified word lists are two specially prepared sets of lists—set "A" and set "B." I use these lists as an aid in the construction of crossword puzzles (or any other type of word puzzles). I use them mostly to find a specific word (or a large number of specific words) easily and quickly in a matter of seconds without the aid of a dictionary.

The classified word lists were compiled and arranged in alphabetical order from all the suitable two-, three-, four-, five-, six-, seven-, and eight-letter words that were found in the four sections of the Merriam-Webster New Collegiate Dictionary. Each list was compiled individually according to the number of letters in each word.

Besides being arranged in alphabetical order, many words in these lists were given a code letter for fast, easy, and efficient definition reference. In addition, each individual classified list of words was indexed so that any specific word (or a large number of specific words) could be located instantly by a mere flick of a finger.

In addition to the regular words and names, the two-, three-, and four-letter lists also contain (arranged in alphabetical order) abbreviations, chemical symbols, prefixes, suffixes, combining form words, and a list of the basic Roman numerals, which I listed on the last page of each individual list of words. They are indicated in the lists by an index tab marked "abbr."

The classified lists of words in set "A," were compiled from all the suitable words in my dictionary. All the words in these lists were arranged and listed in a manner that placed the first letter of each word in alphabetical order, as shown in Figure 1. (This is an exact duplicate of the first page in my classified four-letter list of words in set "A.")

The classified lists of words in set "B," were compiled from all the words that were listed in the "A" set of lists. All the words in the "B" set of lists were arranged and listed in a manner that placed the last two letters of each word in alphabetical order, as shown in Figure 2. (This is also an exact duplicate of the first page in my classified four-letter list of words in set "B.")

Incidentally, I would like to point out that many words in my dictionary were deliberately omitted from my classified lists because they weren't suitable for crossword puzzles. For example, I omitted all words that referred to death, illness, or diseases; unpleasant, offensive, obsolete, archaic, and dialect words. Many other words in my dictionary—even short ones—that were defined by long, difficult, or complicated definitions were also omitted from my classified lists of words.

Before I begin to explain in detail how these classified lists of words came into being, how they were compiled, and how they are used as an aid in the construction of crossword puzzles, I want to point out that it really isn't necessary for you to have these classified lists of words in order to construct crossword puzzles. You can construct all types of word puzzles—with the exception of acrostic puzzles—simply with the aid of an ordinary dictionary.

As a beginner, you don't have to compile these classified lists of words before you start to construct crossword puzzles—at least not at the present time. I suggest, however, that you read this chapter, study it, and when you really decide that you want to construct crossword puzzles for profit rather than just as a hobby, then you can compile your own sets of classified lists of words in your spare time.

When you use the classified lists of words as your source of reference, you can dispense with your dictionary when you work on the diagram sections of your puzzles. You will use your dictionary only to look up certain definitions, or to verify the correct spelling of certain words.

I constructed and sold a large number of puzzles long before I actually became fully aware of the fact that I wasted an enormous amount of valuable time whenever I looked for suitable or specific words in my dictionary. I finally decided that in order to save valuable time and energy, not to mention the wear and tear on my nerves, I would compile my own classified list of two- to eight-letter words. (The reason that I stopped with the eight-letter list of words, is that I very seldom use words in my diagrams that contain more than eight letters.)

I must admit that compiling the classified lists of words was no simple assignment; it was a long, tedious task. By working on these lists only in my spare time, the task took several months to complete. I must also admit that ever since I started to use my classified lists of words as my main source of reference, I have been fully convinced that the time spent compiling them was well worth the effort. The time I now spend to fill in my diagrams, with the aid of my classified lists of words, has been reduced dramatically. A difficult task has been made easy.

The first two rough drafts of my classified lists of words were compiled with a pencil in the following manner:

1. I compiled four separate lists of two-letter words and names from the four sections of my Merriam-Webster New Collegiate Dictionary—the General Vocabulary, the Biographical Names, the Pronouncing Gazetteer, and the Common English Given Names sections.

2. The four separate lists of two-letter words and names were rearranged and listed in alphabetical order, and then they were all combined to form one individual list of two-letter words and names.

3. All the two-letter names that were taken from the last three sections of my dictionary—Biographical Names, Pronouncing Gazetteer, and the Common English Given Names sections—were given code letters for future reference, as shown in the following three examples:

(a) The two-letter name Ae, which, incidentally, was the only two-letter name in the Biographical Names section, was given the code letter "b." Thus, Ae-b ("b" stands for Biographical section).

(b) The two-letter names that were taken from the Pronouncing Gazetteer section (nine names in all) were given the code letter "g." Thus, Bo-g ("g" stands for Gazetteer section).

(c) The two-letter names (actually nicknames), which were taken from the Common English Given Names section, were given the code letters "nn." Thus, Al-nn ("nn" stands for nickname).

(d) Full names such as John, Mary, Albert, etc., which were taken from the Common English Given Names section, were given the code letter "n." Thus, John-n ("n" stands for proper given name).

(The main reason that all the names that were taken from the last three sections of my dictionary were given code letters, was that whenever I wished to look up a specific word, a name, or a definition for a specific word or name, I knew at a glance, by the code letter, in what particular section of my dictionary it was located.)

4. In addition to the regular two-letter words and names, I also compiled (in alphabetical order) a complete list of all the two-letter abbreviations, chemical symbols, prefixes, suffixes, and a list of all the two-letter Roman numerals—II, IV, VI, IX, XI, XV, LI, CI, CL, CC, CD, DC, DI, CM, MI, and MM—which I placed at the end of my two-letter list of classified words.

5. After I had all the two-letter words, names, abbreviations, etc. arranged alphabetically, I typed them all out on clean sheets of paper.

I made a cover for my two-letter list of classified words in a manner as shown in the following two easy steps:

1. I took a clean sheet of typewriter paper on which I printed (with black India ink) the letter "A" and the number 2 (A-2) in medium-sized figures, in eight different places of the cover.

2. In the middle of the upper and the lower half of the cover, I printed identical letters and numbers (A-2) but much larger in size.

The main reason for all the letters and numbers on the covers of all my classified lists of words is that whenever I need a specific list of words which may be mixed up with other lists of classified words, I can find it easily and quickly by looking for the specific identification letter and number on its cover. Even if only a small section of the cover is exposed to view, one of the identification letters and numbers are usually visible. So it's a simple matter for me to pick out the specific list of words I need.

3. I laid the completed cover on top of my two-letter list of classified words and stapled them all together.

(Actually, the two- and the three-letter lists of words were so short that I combined them both to make one individual list of words. Even the combined list of words was so short that it didn't require any index tabs. However, I did make index tabs for all my other lists of classified words.)

I made my index tabs, which I pasted to the bottoms of my classified lists of words, in a manner as shown in the following four easy steps:

1. I took plain index cards (3×5) and cut them into ¾×1¼ index tabs. (Any kind of fairly stiff white paper will serve the same purpose.)

2. I divided the index tabs into two equal sections by a pencil mark.

3. On one end of the index tabs, I printed (with black India ink) the letters of the alphabet.

4. On the opposite ends of the index tabs, I placed a small dab of paste and pasted them to the bottoms of the corresponding pages of my classified lists of words—that is, the "A" index tabs were pasted to the bottoms of the pages that contained the list of words that started with the letter "A." The "B" index tabs were pasted to the bottoms of the pages that contained the list of words that started with the letter "B," etc.

To get a general idea of what the cover of a finished list of classified words looks like, see the illustration in Figure 1. This cover illustration, with the index tabs showing, is actually an illustration of my classified list of five-letter words.

The reason I chose the five-letter list of classified words as an illustrated example instead of the two-letter list, is the fact that all the suitable two-letter words and names that were taken from my dictionary covered only about half a sheet of paper; so, as I have pointed out previously, the combined list of two- and three-letter words was so short that it didn't require any index tabs. On the other hand, the classified list of five-letter words covered twelve full pages; therefore, I chose it as an example, because I felt that it illustrated my point more clearly.

The fact that this particular list of words contained more pages than the combined list of two- and three-letter words, it permitted me to spread the index tabs over a wider range to show a clear-cut view of how they were pasted to the bottoms of the pages of the five-letter list.

Incidentally, you will notice that some of the index tabs contain more than one letter of the alphabet—two, three, or four letters on a single tab. The reason for this is that many single pages in the classified list of words contain several different specific lists of words that start with different letters of the alphabet; therefore, I use two or

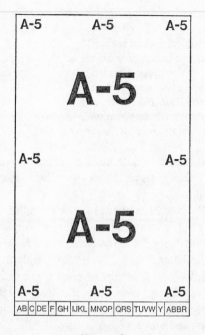

Figure 1

more identification letters on a single index tab to show that a particular page contains more than one specific list of words, and each specific list starts with a different letter of the alphabet.

The remaining six classified lists of three-, four-, five-, six-, seven-, and eight-letter words were compiled and arranged in alphabetical order in exactly the same manner as the two-letter list of words.

Before I start explaining how I use my classified lists of words as an aid in crossword puzzle constructing, I want to make one more point clear.

There were many names in the last three sections of my dictionary that were identical in spelling with many of the words in the General Vocabulary section. Whenever I encountered such an occurrence, I listed both the word (or words) and the name (or names) in my classified lists of words.

The names that were taken from the last three sections of my dictionary were given code letters to distinguish them from the ordinary words that were taken from the General Vocabulary section and bear no code letters.

Examples:

Attar-b   (Biographical Names section)
attar   (General Vocabulary section)
basil   (General Vocabulary section)
Basil-b   (Biographical Names section)
Basil-n   (English Given Name section)
bear   (General Vocabulary section)
Bear-g   (Pronouncing Gazetteer section)

Incidentally, whenever two or more identical words or names appear in my lists, I always select the word or the name that carries the simplest definition.

To find a specific word (or words) in my classified lists of words, I proceed as shown in the following examples: Example 1:

Let's assume that I need a seven-letter word for my diagram that must start with the letter "P_ _ _ _ _ _." I simply flip the index tab marked "P" on my seven-letter list of classified words (A-7), and I have before me, instantly, over four hundred suitable seven-letter words and names to choose from—each word and name is listed in alphabetical order and starts with the letter "P_ _ _ _ _ _." Example 2:

In this example, let's assume that I need a seven-letter word for my diagram that must start with the letters "Pr_ _ _ _ _." A mere flip of the index tab marked "P" on my seven-letter list of classified words (A-7), and in a matter of seconds, I have before me, arranged in alphabetical order, a complete list of all the suitable seven-letter words and names that start with the letters "Pr_ _ _ _ _." (86 words and names.) Example 3:

Let's assume, for example, that I need a six-letter word, that must start with the letters "Tra_ _ _." I simply flip the "T" index tab on my six-letter list of classified words (A-6) and again, in a matter of seconds, I have before me, arranged in alphabetical order, a complete list of all the suitable six-letter words and names that start with the letters "Tra_ _ _." (19 words and names.) Example 4:

In this example, let's assume that I need an an eight-letter word that must start with the letter "D_ _ _ _ _ _ _"; but in addition, the fifth letter of the word must be the letter "L." Thus, "D_ _ _ L_ _ _."

First, I simply flip the "D" index tab on my eight-letter list of classified words (A-8), and in a matter of seconds, I have before me a complete list of all the suitable eight-letter words and names that start with the letter "D_ _ _ _ _ _ _."

Next, in order to pick out all the eight-letter words that contain the letter "L" in the fifth position, I lay the edge of a 12″ ruler in a vertical position alongside the fifth letter of each word in the "D" column of words. Then simply by glancing at the fifth letter of each word (the letter alongside the ruler), I can quickly scan and pick out all the eight-letter words that start with the letter "D" and also contain the letter "L" in the fifth position of the words.

This particular operation, complicated as it may seem, takes only a few minutes to perform, and it gives me eleven suitable words to choose from—dandlers, dangling, dawdlers, demolish, derelict, develops, diddlers, displace, displays, doubloon, and dwelling.

The preceding examples clearly show that I can—and do—make greater progress in crossword puzzle constructing when I use my own classified lists of words as my source of reference instead of my dictionary.

To illustrate a more specific example, let's assume that I need a four-letter word for my diagram that must start with the letter "S_ _ _."

If I use my dictionary as my source of reference from which I must select a list of these specific four-letter words, I must search through 119 pages of the General Vocabulary; in addition, I must look over more than 5,000 individual words in order to pick out only the four-letter words that start with the letter "S_ _ _." And this, of course, doesn't include the four-letter names in the Biographical section, the Pronouncing Gazetteer, and the Common English Given Names section.

Of course, I must admit that I have never timed myself in a test such as this. I do know, however, that such an assignment can't be completed in a few seconds. But . . . if I use my own four-letter list of classified words (A-4) as my source of reference, I can have, in a matter of seconds, a complete list of all the suitable four-letter words and names—from the four sections of my dictionary—that start with the letter "S_ _ _" merely by a flip of the "S" index tab on my four-letter list of classified words.

I believe the preceding examples are convincing enough to prove that my own method for finding suitable words for my diagrams is fast, accurate, and efficient. This method works extremely well for me, and I see no reason in the world why it will not work for you as well.

My first set of classified lists of words ("A" set) produced such wonderful results that I decided to compile an entirely new set of classified lists of words which I called my "B" set of lists.

I compiled my "B" set of classified lists of words in a manner so that the last two letters of each word were arranged and listed in alphabetical order, as opposed to the first letter of each word in my "A" set of lists.

All the words in my "B" set of lists were compiled from the lists of words in my "A" set. Each individual list of words in my "B" set was compiled separately but in the same manner.

To illustrate the method I used to compile my classified lists of words in my "B" set, I use my four-letter list of words as an example, because with this particular list, I believe that I can illustrate my method more clearly, more efficiently, and more effectively.

The first draft of my four-letter list of classified words in my "B" set was compiled with a pencil in the following manner:

1. Starting at the top of my four-letter list of classified words in my "A" set (A-4), I compiled, in alphabetical order, a list of all the four-letter words and names that ended with the letter "A." When the entire list was completed, I laid it aside for the time being.

2. Again, starting at the top of my four-letter list of classified words in the "A" set (A-4), I compiled, in alphabetical order, a list of all the four-letter words and names that ended with the letter "B." When this list was completed, I also laid it aside for the time being.

In this manner I continued through the alphabet. When all the four-letter words and names from my "A-4" list of classified words were compiled according to the remaining letters of the alphabet, I started on my second draft of the four-letter words.

I took the first list of four-letter words (step 1) that ended with the letter "A," and rearranged the words in this particular list so that the last two letters of each word were arranged in alphabetical order, as shown in the following examples:

(a) Starting at the top of the "A" list of words (step 1), I first looked for four-letter words ending in "＿＿aa." Since there were none, I went onto words ending in "＿＿ba."

(b) Again, starting at the top of the "A" list of words (step 1), I compiled and arranged in alphabetical order a complete list of all the

four-letter words and names that ended with the letters "_ _ba"—
Cuba-g, Elba-g, and reba (see Figure 2).

(c) Again, starting at the top of the "A" list of words (step 1), I
compiled and arranged in alphabetical order a complete list of all the
four-letter words and names that ended with the letters "_ _ca"—
deca, Inca, loca, paca, and pica (see Figure 2).

(d) I followed the same procedure to compile and arrange in alphabetical order a complete list of all the remaining four-letter words
and names in the "A" list (step 1) that ended with the letters
"_ _da," "_ _ea," "_ _fa," "_ _ga," "_ _ha," etc.

I followed the same procedure to compile and arrange in alphabetical order all the four-letter words and names from the "B" list of
words (step 2) that ended with the letters "_ _ab"—Ahab, arab,
blab, crab, drab, Moab-g, Raab-g, slab, and swab.

Next, I compiled a list of all the four-letter words and names that
ended with the letters "_ _bb"—bibb, Cobb-b.

And then I compiled a list of all the four-letter words and names
that ended with the letters "_ _eb"—bleb. (There was only one
four-letter word that ended with these two letters.)

I worked so on down the line for all the remaining letters of the
alphabet (see Figure 2).

Study Figure 2. It will give you a fairly accurate idea of the way I
compiled and listed in alphabetical order all the remaining four-letter
words and names in my "B" list. In fact, it will give you a general
idea of the way that the remaining six lists of words in my "B" set
were compiled.

I would like to point out that when I began to arrange in alphabetical order the last two letters of each word and name in my "B"
set of lists, I started at the top of the list for each letter of the
alphabet. This procedure placed not only the last two letters of each
word and name in alphabetical order but also the first two letters of
each word and name.

The two- to eight-letter lists of classified words in my "B" set were
compiled in the same manner.

When the second draft of all the words in my "B" set of lists were
compiled and arranged in alphabetical order, I typed each individual
list of classified words on clean sheets of paper. Next, I made an individual cover for each list and stapled them together.

To complete the lists, I provided each list with suitable index tabs.

With the aid of my classified lists of words in the "B" set, I can

A	Baia-g	Iona-g	Casa	Ahab	Stub	Eyed	Mild
Cuba-g		Lana-n	Casa-g	Arab		Feed	Mold
Elba-g	Baja-g	Lena-n	Lisa-n	Blab	Brac	Fled	Sold
Reba-g	Raja	Luna	Mesa	Crab		Fred-nn	Wild
	Mana		Musa-g	Drab	Alec-nn	Heed	Wold
Deca	Deka	Mina	Nysa-g	Grab		Hued	
Inca	Kaka	Mona-n	Rosa-n	Moab-g	Bric	Iced	Band
Loca	Pika	Nina-n	Ursa	Raab-g	Chic	Lied	Bend
Paca		Pina	Vasa-g	Slab	Epic	Meed	Bind
Pica	Bola	Rena-n	Visa	Swab	Eric-n	Need	Bond
	Cola	Tina-nn			Laic	Pied	Bund
Aida	Fula	Tuna	Acta	Bibb	Odic	Pled	Fend
Alda-b	Gala	Ulna	Anta	Cobb-b	Otic	Reed	Find
Coda	Hyla	Vena	Beta			Reed-b	Fond
Edda	Hula	Vina	Cata	Bleb	Bloc	Seed	Fund
Leda-n	Kula-g	Yana-n	Etta-n		Floc	Shed	Gand-g
Soda	Lola-n		Gata	Crib		Sled	Hand
Vida-b	Mola-b	Proa	Iota	Glib	Marc	Sned	Hind
	Olla	Shoa-g	Meta	Guib		Sped	Kind
Acea	Pula	Stoa	Nita-nn		Disc	Sued	Land
Area	Sala-g		Octa	Bulb	Fisc	Toed	Lend
Asea	Sola	Napa-g	Oeta-g			Used	Lind-b
Flea	Tola	Nipa	Pita	Bomb	Arad-g	Weed	Mind
Gaea	Tula-g	Papa	Rita-n	Comb	Bead		Pend
Idea	Vela	Pupa	Rota	Dumb	Brad	Amid	Rand-b
Plea	Vila-g		Seta	Jamb	Clad	Arid	Rend
Rhea		Agra-g		Lamb	Egad	Avid-n	Rind
Uvea	Alma	Apra	Aqua	Lamb-b	Glad	Enid	Sand
Thea	Alma-n	Aura		Limb	Goad	Grid	Send
	Alma-g	Bora	Alva-b	Numb	Head	Laid	Tend
Sofa	Bema	Cora-n	Deva		Lead	Maid	Vend
Tufa	Boma-g	Dora-n	Diva	Blob	Load	Ovid-b	Wand
	Cyma	Ezra-n	Elva-n	Boob	Read	Paid	Wend
Alga	Duma-b	Hera	Java-g	Knob	Road	Raid	Wind
Mega	Emma-n	Jura-g	Kava	Slob	Shad	Said	
Olga-n	Hama-g	Kura-g	Kiva	Swob	Thad	Skid	Clod
Ruga	Kama-g	Lyra	Neva-g	Curb	Woad	Void	Food
Saga	Lima	Mora	Sava-g	Garb			Good
Toga	Lima-g	Myra-n	Suva-g	Herb	Judd-b	Auld	Hood
Vega	Mama	Nara-g	Viva	Serb	Kidd-b	Bald	Mood
Yoga	Puma	Nora-n		Sorb	Lidd-b	Beld	Plod
	Soma	Para	Biwa	Verb	Rudd	Bold	Pood
Haha	Yuma-g	Para-g	Iowa-g			Cold	Prod
Naha-g		Sara-n	Nawa-g	Chub	Aged	Fold	Rood
	Anna-n	Sera		Club	Abed	Gild	Shod
Apia	Cana-g	Sora	Hexa	Daub	Aped	Gold	Snod
Aria	Dana-b	Sura		Drub	Bred	Held	Trod
Aria-g	Dona-n	Vara	Gaya-g	Grub	Coed	Hold	Wood
Asia-g	Duna-g	Vera-n	Maya	Snub	Deed	Meld	Wood-b

Figure 2

find a specific word—or a list of specific words—that ends with a specific letter—or letters—easily and quickly in a matter of seconds.

I use my classified lists of words in the "B" set in the following manner.

Suppose I need a suitable four-letter word for my diagram that must end with the letter "_ _ _r." I simply flip the "R" index tab on my four-letter list of classified words (B-4); and, instantly, I have before me—arranged in alphabetical order—a complete list of all the suitable four-letter words and names that end with the letter "_ _ _r"—a total of 87 suitable words and names arranged in the following order: 27, ending with the letters "_ _ar"; 22, with the letters "_ _er"; 1 name that ends with the letters "_ _hr"; 13 words and names that end with the letters "_ _ir"; 7, with the letters "_ _or"; and 9 words that end with the letters "_ _ur."

Or let's assume, for example, that I want a complete list of all four-letter words and names that end with the letter "_ _ _o." With a mere flip of the "O" index tab on my four-letter list of classified words (B-4), I have before me, instantly, 107 suitable four-letter words and names—arranged in alphabetical order—that end with the letter "_ _ _o." I must admit that this is quite an impressive number of words and names to choose from.

I would like to point out, however, that if I were to compile an identical list of four-letter words and names from my dictionary, I would have to check every single page, every single word, and every single name in my dictionary—a total of approximately 137,000 words and names. A task such as this would require practically a full day to complete. However, by using my four-letter list of classified words (B-4) as my source of reference, I have an identical list of four-letter words and names (total of 107) merely with a flick of my finger.

HOW CROSSWORD PUZZLES ARE CLASSIFIED

Crossword puzzles, as a rule, are divided into three simple classifications—simple, medium, and difficult. However, in some crossword puzzle magazines, you may find two additional classifications—beginner's and very difficult puzzles.

For simplicity, throughout this book, I will use the editors' terms to classify puzzles. I will simply refer to them as easy, medium, and difficult.

Easy crossword puzzles usually contain familiar words in the diagram section—simple words that are used in everyday language—and proportionately easy definitions.

As a rule, you will find that the majority of the easy crossword puzzles do not include foreign words, mythological names, obsolete or archaic words in the diagram sections of their puzzles. However, this isn't a set rule. Occasionally you may find a few difficult or foreign words in the diagram sections of some easy puzzles. It all depends, of course, on the editor's point of view. Most editors set up their own particular rules about the use of certain words in their puzzles.

I might also point out that there are some editors who will not accept archaic or obsolete words under any kind of condition or in any kind of crossword puzzle—easy, medium, or difficult.

Whenever you're compelled to use difficult words in the diagram sections of your puzzles—and many times you can't avoid them—be sure to cross the difficult words with easy ones.

The medium puzzles, if they are constructed according to the rules, are neither too easy nor too difficult to solve. You will find, however, that the majority of the words in the diagram sections of the medium puzzles and the definitions for these words are usually slanted toward the easy side. And, of course, a few difficult words or a few difficult definitions are added to the puzzles to give them an added bit of spice, so to speak.

The difficult puzzles, on the other hand, contain difficult words in the diagram sections of the puzzles, or they may contain difficult definitions, or they may contain a combination of both difficult words and difficult definitions.

Usually, but not as a rule, you will find that the majority of the larger size puzzles—17×17, 19×19, 21×21, and 23×23—fall into the difficult classification. However, don't let the above statement fool you completely, because it's also quite possible to construct smaller size puzzles that can be classified as difficult.

And I might also add that it's quite possible to transform an easy puzzle into a difficult one simply by changing the definitions from easy to difficult.

To illustrate a point, study the following two columns of definitions. The first column is composed of easy definitions, and the second column is composed of difficult definitions.

(Before you look at the answers to both columns of definitions, see if you can fill in the proper words to match the definitions in both columns.)

    Column ⚹1:
1. Metallic rock   ——
2. Skillet   ——
3. Fishing pole   ——
4. Disfigures   ——
5. Biblical garden   ——
6. Parcel of land   ——
7. French capital   ——
8. Raced on foot   ——
9. Name   ——
10. Feline pet   ——

    Column ⚹2:
1. Danish bronze   ——
2. God of the flocks   ——
3. Aaron's miracle worker   ——
4. Roman god of war   ——
5. Blissful abode   ——
6. Abraham's nephew   ——
7. Achille's slayer   ——
8. Aegir's wife   ——
9. Agnomen   ——
10. Anchor tackle   ——

Figure 3

Answers: (The answers to both columns of definitions are identical.) 1. ore, 2. pan, 3. rod, 4. mars, 5. eden, 6. lot, 7. Paris, 8. ran, 9. title, 10. cat.

I would like to point out the fact that all puzzles—large or small—don't always turn out the way that you want them. There will be many times—and you can bet on that—when you will begin to construct easy or medium puzzles and end up with difficult ones. The reason for the change in the classifications—from easy or medium to difficult—is rather difficult to explain.

All the troubles seem to be caused by the way that certain words fit into your diagrams. Certain combinations of letters can often force you to use difficult words in your diagrams. Whenever you find yourself being forced to use difficult words in the diagram section of your puzzle (especially when you intend to construct an easy or a medium puzzle), erase a few of the last words entered in your diagram and try a new approach with different words. If the different words in your diagram don't solve your problem, erase a few more words from your diagram and try again. If the second attempt does not solve your problem, erase all the words from your diagram and start again from the beginning—unless, of course, you're working on a large 23×23 puzzle.

If you really want to become a successful crossword puzzle constructor and contributor, and if you want to sell many of your puzzles to the editors of crossword puzzle magazines, I strongly suggest that you construct most of your puzzles as easy or medium puzzles in the smaller sizes—11×11, 13×13 and 15×15.

You probably will find through your own experience, as I did, that the smaller size crossword puzzles that are classified as easy or as medium puzzles seem to be accepted more readily for publication by the editors of crossword puzzle magazines in preference over the larger size puzzles or the difficult ones.

I suggest that you study many crossword puzzle magazines thoroughly before you attempt to construct and submit any puzzles. I'm sure you will find that most of the puzzles in these magazines are of the smaller sizes and in the easy or the medium classification. In fact, you'll find that the easier you make your puzzles, the better chance they will have of being accepted. On the other hand, do not overlook or neglect the larger size puzzles or the difficult ones. After all, there is a limit as to the number of smaller size puzzles that an editor can afford to buy in a single month.

Many times editors do get overstocked with certain sizes or certain types of puzzles; therefore, from time to time, offer them a variety of puzzles to choose from. Occasionally, submit a few of the larger size puzzles together with your smaller size ones. And don't forget the difficult puzzles; submit one or two of them occasionally with your easy or medium puzzles. And remember, too, that your larger size puzzles will stand a very much better chance of being accepted for publication if you construct them as easy or medium puzzles.

Give the editors the types and the sizes of crossword puzzles that they want and need, and you will not encounter any difficulty in selling them.

And while I'm still on the subject of puzzle classifications and sizes, I would like to point out one more important fact.

Many beginners are under the false impression that they can earn more money if they construct and sell the larger size puzzles because the rates for these puzzles are much higher than the rates for the smaller size. Let me assure you, however, that actually the opposite is true. The fact is that you can construct three small 13×13 size puzzles in a shorter period of time than it takes to construct one large 23×23 puzzle. Furthermore, three 13×13 puzzles bring in more money than one 23×23 puzzle.

As a rule, most requirement sheets will inform you as to the types and the sizes of crossword puzzles that the editors wish to purchase. However, if the requirement sheets don't contain this bit of information (and many of them don't), then I suggest that you study the publishers' crossword puzzle magazines to obtain whatever necessary information may be lacking in their requirement sheets.

Of course, experienced crossword puzzle constructors can usually acquire the necessary information they need in order to construct the types of puzzles that certain publications want simply by studying the puzzles and the formats in the publishers' magazines. For the beginners, however, it's rather a difficult task, because most beginners aren't too familiar with the publishers' formats.

II How to Draw Diagrams

As a crossword puzzle constructor, the first things that you will need in order to construct these puzzles (or any other types of word puzzles) are blank crossword puzzle diagrams.

Unfortunately, I don't know anyone who prints and sells blank crossword puzzle diagrams. Someday perhaps a few venturesome printers may be persuaded to print them, but in the meantime, you must learn to draw your own diagrams.

The size of the crossword puzzle diagram (which really is the puzzle size) is determined by the number of squares (sometimes called blocks) in a single row of squares running horizontally and by the number of squares in a single row of squares running vertically. For example, a 9×9 diagram is nine squares wide and nine squares deep. A 13×13 size diagram is thirteen squares wide and thirteen squares deep, etc.

As a rule, practically all the crossword puzzles that are found in most crossword puzzle magazines are constructed with diagrams that are symmetrical (square) in form—that is, each diagram contains an equal number of squares on all four sides. This rule, however, isn't a fixed rule. Occasionally, you may find an odd-sized diagram in some crossword puzzle magazines. In fact, one publisher uses several 19×15 size puzzles each month in one of his magazines. And you may find that many of the smaller size puzzles that are published in many of the daily newspapers also have odd-sized diagrams.

In order to construct professional-looking puzzles, you must start with properly drawn diagrams. If the squares in the diagrams are incorrectly spaced, or improperly drawn, the typed numbers and the words will not line-up properly. Whenever situations such as these occur, the diagram pages lose their professional-looking quality.

If you follow the instructions carefully and precisely in this chapter, you will find that it's quite simple to draw crossword puzzle diagrams. Keep in mind the fact that these instructions apply to all diagram sizes—for large or small diagrams, the instructions and the drawing procedure remain the same.

Before I explain the drawing procedure for diagrams, I would like to point out that before you start to draw them, you must first locate the starting points for the diagrams on the diagram pages.

The starting points will automatically place the diagram outlines in the proper areas on the diagram pages. If this bit of information has you somewhat confused at this point, don't worry too much about it; it will all clear itself up in the following chapter when you will be shown how to locate the starting points for the diagrams on the diagram pages. I suggest that you also read that chapter before you attempt to draw crossword puzzle diagrams. It will give you a clearer idea of the basic rules that you must follow in order to draw professional-looking diagrams.

The idea of using the typewriter as an accurate spacing device came about when I discovered—after I drew my first diagrams—that I couldn't type the numbers and the letters of the words properly in the small squares of my diagrams, because the small squares in the diagrams were improperly spaced. However, ever since I started to use the typewriter as an accurate spacing device, I'm happy to say that all the numbers and all the words fit perfectly into the individual squares of my diagrams.

I draw each diagram—regardless of size—in three easy stages. First, I outline the diagram with dots; next, I divide the outlined diagram into small individual squares; and then, I ink in solid all the unused squares (black squares) in the diagram.

In the diagram illustrations, as shown in Figures 4, 5, and 6, I use small 9×9 diagrams to illustrate the method I use to draw diagrams, because the four small diagrams fit perfectly on a single page. Therefore, I can show the twelve illustrations on three pages instead of twelve.

Before you attempt to draw any diagrams, you must remember two

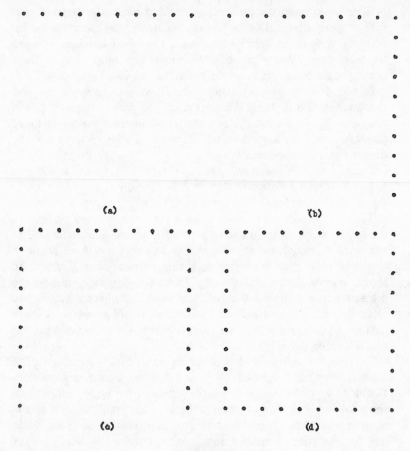

Figure 4

important facts when outlining the diagrams with dots. First, you must remember to allow three spaces between all the dots in the diagram outlines that run in the horizontal positions. Second, you must remember to allow two spaces between all the dots in the diagram outlines that run in the vertical positions.

In order to draw a complete diagram design, follow the instructions as directed in the following eleven steps:

1. Insert a blank sheet of paper into the typewriter and type a series of ten triple-spaced dots in the horizontal position as shown in Figure 4-a. (The sheet of paper on which you draw the diagram is

called the diagram page.)

2. Drop down two spaces (directly in line with the last dot) and type a series of nine double-spaced dots in the vertical position, as shown in Figure 4-b.

3. Roll the diagram page back to the first dot of the diagram outline.

4. Drop down two spaces (directly in line with the first dot), and type a series of nine double-spaced dots in the vertical position, as shown in Figure 4-c.

5. Type in the remaining eight triple-spaced dots at the bottom of the diagram outline, as shown in Figure 4-d. This step completes the basic outline of the diagram.

The rule for triple spacing between horizontal dots and double spacing between vertical dots in the diagram outline holds true for all types of diagrams with the exception of diagrams for acrostic puzzles.

6. Remove the diagram page (outlined diagram) from the typewriter.

7. With the aid of a steel-edged ruler and a fountain pen, draw eight vertical lines on the diagram page between the upper and the lower rows of horizontal dots, as shown in Figure 5-b. (Work from right to left—assuming, of course, that you're right-handed. If you're left-handed, you'll find it more practical and convenient to work from left to right.)

8. Give the diagram page a quarter turn to the right—or to the left—and draw eight horizontal lines between the left and the right row of vertical dots, as shown in Figure 5-c.

9. To complete the outside squares in the diagram, draw the remaining four outer lines, as shown in Figure 5-d. (Draw the four outer lines in the diagram slightly heavier than the rest of the diagram. Without removing the ruler, retrace each outer line several times with a fountain pen.

10. With a pencil, mark an X in every unused square (black square) in the diagram, as shown in Figure 6-a.

11. Use a small artist's brush and black waterproof India ink to ink in solid each square in the diagram that is marked with an X.

Whether you work on a single diagram or several diagrams at one time, you will find it most practical to ink in the unused squares in four easy steps, as shown in Figures 6-a, b, c, and d. When you use this method, the ink has a much better chance to dry between each step, and your diagrams will not become ink-smudged in case they

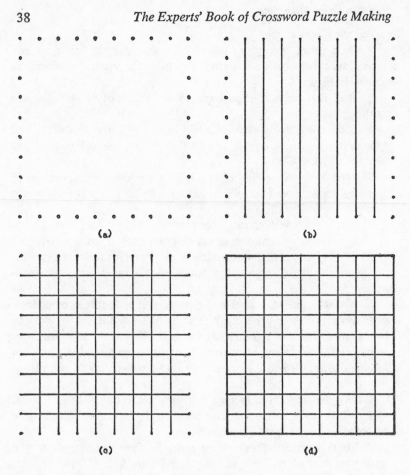

(a) (b)

(c) (d)

Figure 5

are moved around accidentally while the ink is still wet.

A complete diagram, with all the unused squares inked in solid, is called a diagram design. To change a diagram design, you simply rearrange the black squares in the diagram. To duplicate a diagram design, you ink in all the black squares in the diagram in exactly the same manner as you find them in the original diagram design.

Before you start to ink in the unused squares in the diagram, recheck all the squares that are marked with an X just to be absolutely sure that all the X's are marked in their correct squares. If you find an X marked in an incorrect square, it's a simple matter to erase

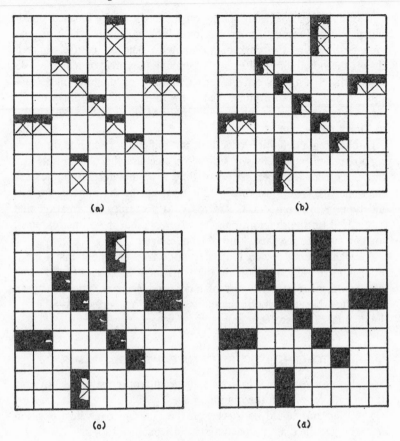

Figure 6

the X from the incorrect square and move it over to the correct
square. On the other hand, if you ink in the incorrect squares in the
diagram, it will be ruined. You will have to discard the diagram and
draw a new one.

Get in the habit of rechecking all of your material—the words in
the diagram, the definitions, spelling, etc. Be on the lookout, particularly, for misspelled words in the diagram section of the puzzle. The
few extra minutes that you spend rechecking your material may save
you an hour of extra work—especially if you discover an error in the
rough stage of the puzzle.

Too many heavy erasure marks on the surface of a finished puzzle will produce a smudgy, unprofessional-looking puzzle which an editor may brand as the work of an amateur. And, of course, there is always the possibility that excessive erasing may mar or tear the delicate surface of the paper. A torn definition or diagram page in a finished puzzle is unfortunate, because you probably will have to discard the torn section of the puzzle—diagram or definition page—and construct a new one.

Duplicating a definition page isn't too difficult a task; it is duplicating a diagram page that is troublesome, because the diagram, as you know, requires a longer period of time to complete. To duplicate a diagram page, you must draw a diagram, ink in the unused squares, and type in the numbers, the words, and necessary information that is required on the diagram page. And even then, if you get careless, you can run into the same kind of trouble again.

A clean-looking puzzle that is smudge free and contains a minimum number of errors is truly the work of a professional. So don't take any unnecessary chances of having your puzzle rejected by an editor just because you're careless. Strive for perfection—the ultimate goal of all professionals.

HOW TO CENTER THE DIAGRAM ON THE DIAGRAM PAGE

Now that you've learned to draw a diagram, you must also learn how to place it properly on the diagram page.

The diagram should be placed on the diagram page in a position that will give the diagram page a pleasing, balanced look.

I know of no specific rule to follow for placing the diagram on the diagram page. You will find, however, that if you place the diagram in the lower section of the diagram page in a manner so that the margins on the three lower sides of the diagram—the right side, the left side, and the bottom—are all equally spaced, the diagram page takes on a fairly balanced look.

When you place the diagram in the lower section of the diagram page, you will have more blank space above the diagram for your name, address, source of reference, and word count—if it is requested. In addition, the editor who buys your puzzle will also be happy to find more blank space above the diagram for his notes or comments.

In order to place the diagram in the proper position on the

diagram page, you must first locate the starting point for the diagram.

Incidentally, the starting point is nothing more than an ordinary dot that is located in a specific spot on the diagram page. This dot is actually the point from which you start to outline the diagram—the spot where you type the first dot for the diagram outline.

When I first started to draw diagrams, I used to locate the starting points for my diagrams with the aid of a ruler. I must admit that it was a rather slow method. But then I eventually hit upon the idea of using a master diagram as a means of locating the starting points for my diagrams on the diagram pages. And now, with the aid of a master diagram, I can locate the starting points on the diagram pages in a matter of seconds.

The master diagram is nothing more than a copied outline of a regular crossword puzzle diagram that has been positioned correctly on the diagram page. It is simple to draw and just as simple to use.

I suggest that you draw a master diagram for every size and every type of word puzzle you intend to construct. Once you learn how to use them, you will never start any diagrams without them.

In order to draw a master diagram for a 13×13 crossword puzzle, follow the nine easy steps as outlined in the following instructions:

1. Take a clean sheet of typewriter paper, and outline (with dots) a 13×13 diagram, as instructed in the previous section. (At this point, don't worry about positioning the diagram correctly on the diagram page.)

2. Remove the outlined diagram from the typewriter and draw only the four outside lines of the diagram, as shown in Figure 8.

3. Take a pair of scissors and cut out the diagram along the four lines of the square. Lay the diagram aside for the time being.

4. Take a clean sheet of typewriter paper and lay it flat on a table or a desk. With the aid of a pencil and a 12″ ruler, lightly draw a diagonal line (on a 45-degree angle) from the lower right-hand corner of the sheet of paper to a point 8½″ up from the bottom on the left-hand side, as shown in Figure 7. (For the purpose of identification, I call this sheet of paper the master diagram page.)

5. Take the cut-out diagram (step 3) and lay it on top of the master diagram page in a position so that the upper left-hand corner and the lower right-hand corner of the cut-out diagram fall exactly on the diagonal line, as shown in Figure 7.

6. Move the cut-out diagram up or down along the diagonal line to a point where the three lower margins—the right-side margin, the

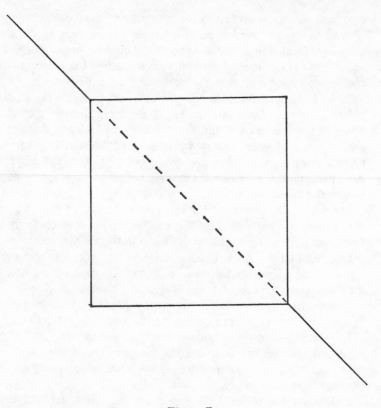

Figure 7

left-side margin and the bottom margin—are equally spaced, as shown in Figure 7.

7. Without disturbing the cut-out diagram, take a sharp-pointed pencil and draw four dots on the master diagram page—one dot at each corner of the cut-out diagram.

8. Remove the cut-out diagram and draw four lines (with pen and ink) between the four dots on the master diagram page to form a square, as shown in Figure 7. (Go over each outline several times with the pen and ink to produce a dark, bold outline.)

9. Erase the penciled diagonal line on the master diagram page and you have a finished 13×13 master diagram, as shown in Figure 8.

This master diagram will help you to locate the proper position on the diagram page for the starting point for a 13×13 diagram.

Figure 8

In order to use the master diagram properly, follow the six easy steps in the following instructions:

1. Lay the master diagram face up on a table or desk.

2. Take a clean sheet of typewriter paper and lay it directly over the master diagram. (For identification purposes, I call this sheet of paper the diagram page.)

3. Line up the four edges of both sheets of paper—pick them up and tap them gently (edgewise) on a table or desk.

4. Now lay both lined-up sheets of paper—the diagram page and the master diagram—face up on a table or desk, and notice how the lines of the master diagram show through the clean sheet of paper— the diagram page.

5. Take a sharp-pointed pencil and draw four dots on the diagram page—one dot at each corner of the master diagram where it shows through the diagram page.

6. Remove the top sheet of paper (diagram page) from the master diagram. And now, you have four pencil dots that form a square on the diagram page.

The upper left-hand dot is the starting point for the diagram on the diagram page. This particular dot is the most important one of the four dots. I refer to it simply as the starting point. The other three dots are of secondary importance; they merely act as automatic stops when you're outlining a diagram.

With these four dots properly placed on the diagram page, you don't have to count the number of dots that make up the complete diagram outline. As long as you keep the diagram outline within the area of these four dots, you can't go wrong; your diagram will always contain the correct number of small squares.

Incidentally, I would like to point out the fact that regardless of the length of time it takes to explain this particular method, which I use (and recommend) for locating the starting point on the diagram page, let me assure you that with the aid of a master diagram, it takes only about five seconds to complete this procedure. Furthermore, this same procedure for locating the starting point for the diagram on the diagram page holds true for all sizes of diagrams—that is, with the proper master diagram for each size.

To outline your diagram with dots, after you have located the starting point on the diagram page, follow the five easy steps as outlined in the following instructions:

1. Insert the diagram page into the typewriter.
2. Release the paper lock on the typewriter so that you can move the diagram page freely in any direction—right, left, up, or down.
3. Place the starting point (on the diagram page) in a position in the typewriter carriage so that when you strike the "period" key on the typewriter keyboard, the period will strike exactly on the starting point on the diagram page—the first dot in the diagram outline.
4. Square up the diagram page, and lock the paper lock to prevent the diagram page from moving around in the typewriter.
5. Now proceed to outline the diagram, as instructed in the preceding section (Figure 4-a, b, c, and d).

If you find that your diagram outline is off to one side a fraction of an inch, don't worry about it too much. No one is going to measure the margins of your diagram page just to see whether they are equally spaced. Draw the diagram as near as you possibly can to the proper position on the diagram page, and let it go at that.

Actually, all the preceding instructions are quite simple to follow, as you will find when you draw a few diagrams. In fact, you will learn to draw diagrams quickly, accurately, and automatically without any fuss or bother, and without any reference to the instructions.

I would like to point out that it actually takes me only about five seconds to position the starting point (on the diagram page) in the proper position in the typewriter. So you see; it really isn't a very difficult operation. And with a little bit of practice, you can really do it as well as I, and in the same length of time.

HOW TO DRAW VARIATION DIAGRAMS

As you become familiar with the different types of word puzzles and diagrams that are published in puzzle magazines, perhaps you will notice that occasionally some of the crossword puzzle diagrams are drawn without any outside black squares (unused squares) showing in the diagram designs, as shown in Figure 10. (Incidentally, these types of diagram designs don't change the basic structure of the crossword puzzle.)

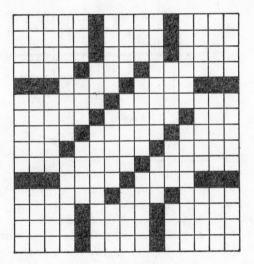

Figure 9

Occasionally you may find a crossword puzzle magazine—and there are several of them—in which the publisher uses this type of diagram exclusively. However, the fact that a publisher uses this type of diagram design in his magazine doesn't necessarily mean that you must include a similar diagram design with the crossword puzzle that you submit.

Regardless of the different types of diagram designs that you may find in different crossword puzzle magazines, unless you are instructed otherwise, use regular crossword puzzle diagram designs for the puzzles you submit. The regular diagram designs are much easier to draw than the variation types, and they will serve adequately.

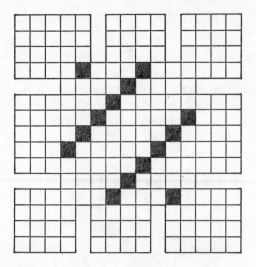

Figure 10

Even though you may never be called upon to draw any diagram designs as shown in Figure 10, or even though you may never have the desire to use them with your crossword puzzles, I think that you should at least know how to draw them. Someday you may want to use a few of these diagram designs with your crossword puzzles for some special reason—perhaps to impress some new editor and prove that you're no amateur in this field.

But before you get carried away with this idea, let me assure you that they may impress an editor but they will not sell uninteresting puzzles. Interesting, clean, professional-looking puzzles will sell with any type of diagram design.

The procedure for drawing this particular diagram design, as shown in Figure 10, is somewhat different from that of an ordinary diagram design. To draw this particular type of diagram design, you must always remember that the starting points for the horizontal and the vertical lines in the diagram are determined by the depth of the outside unused squares (black squares).

You will notice in Figure 9—the regular diagram design—that the depth of the outside unused squares is three squares deep on all four sides of the diagram. Therefore, the starting points for the horizontal and the vertical lines in the diagram design, as shown in Figure 10, are three squares in from each side of the diagram—right side, left side, top, and bottom.

To duplicate the diagram design, as shown in Figure 10, follow the eight easy steps, as outlined in the following instructions.

1. In the usual manner, outline (with dots) an ordinary 15×15 size diagram (Figure 11).

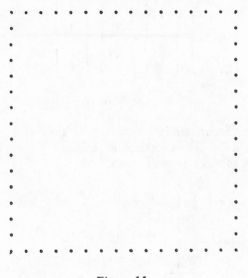

Figure 11

2. With a metal-edged ruler, a fountain pen, and black waterproof ink, draw ten vertical lines between the upper and the lower rows of horizontal dots in the diagram outline, as shown in Figure 12. (Start the vertical lines three squares in from the right side of the diagram outline and three squares in from the left side of the diagram outline. And keep in mind the fact that the space between two dots represents one square in the diagram.

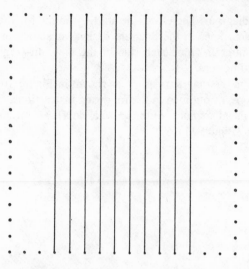

Figure 12

3. Draw ten horizontal lines between the right and the left rows of vertical dots in the diagram outline, as shown in Figure 13. (Start the horizontal lines three squares down from the top of the diagram

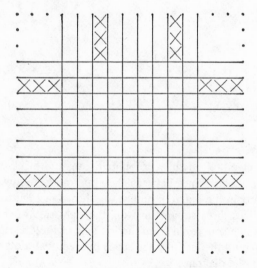

Figure 13

outline and three squares up from the bottom of the diagram outline.)

4. Mark an X, very lightly, with a pencil in each space where the outside unused squares (black squares) should ordinarily be located, as shown in Figure 13.

5. Draw eight additional lines, as shown in Figure 14—two vertical

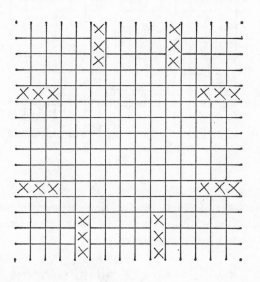

Figure 14

lines on each side of the diagram and two horizontal lines at the top of the diagram and two at the bottom. (When you draw these eight lines, be absolutely sure to skip each outside blank space in the diagram that is marked with an X.)

6. Draw the remaining outside lines, as shown in Figure 15, to complete the diagram.

7. Erase all the pencil-marked X's from the outside blank spaces in the diagram, and you will find that the diagram is identical with the diagram that is shown in Figure 15.

8. Mark and ink in all the remaining unused squares in the diagram, and the finished diagram design will be identical with the diagram design that is shown in Figure 10.

And that's all there is to drawing this particular type of diagram

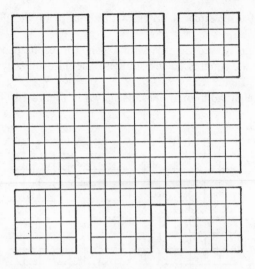

Figure 15

design. You can apply this same method to any size diagram—large or small. Just keep in mind the fact that the starting points for the horizontal and the vertical lines in the diagram are determined by the depth of the outside unused squares.

HOW TO DRAW ODD-SHAPED DIAGRAMS

Occasionally, as you study different publishers' crossword puzzle magazines, you may find a few puzzles in which the diagrams are odd-shaped—that is, the diagrams are not symmetrical (Figure 16).

Aside from the odd-shaped diagrams, there isn't anything special or different about these kinds of crossword puzzles. And regardless of the names that some editors or puzzle constructors wish to give them, they still remain regular crossword puzzles and are constructed as such.

Many editors of crossword puzzle magazines welcome odd-shaped puzzles for their magazines. The reason you don't see too many of them published is, perhaps, that the editors don't receive as many of them as they would like. This, of course, is just a guess on my part.

Odd-shaped diagram designs aren't too difficult to draw, and they could mean more sales for your puzzles. So don't hesitate to experiment with them.

You can obtain many odd-shaped diagram designs from crossword puzzle magazines, or you can design your own. I suggest, however, that you select the diagram designs for your puzzles from the cross-word puzzle magazines of the publishers to whom you intend to submit your puzzles. This way you will at least be sure that whatever diagram designs you select have been approved and accepted by the editor of this particular publication, and that they will meet his standard. Besides, it's much easier to copy a diagram design than to create a new one.

I would like to point out that many of the diagram designs that are used for diagramless crossword puzzles (see the answer pages at the back of the magazines) can also be used as diagrams for odd-shaped crossword puzzles.

At first, the odd-shaped diagram design, as shown in Figure 16, may appear to be somewhat difficult to draw, but don't let that scare you. Every different type of diagram design seems to be difficult to draw—at first. However, when you complete one diagram design, you will find that it isn't nearly as difficult to draw as it may appear. The only noticeable difference in drawing the odd-shaped diagram design, as opposed to the regular diagram design, is the time element —the odd-shaped diagram design requires a longer period of time to complete.

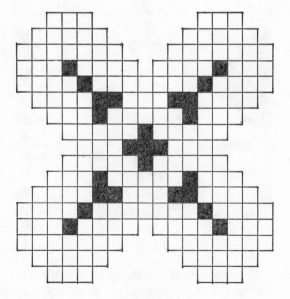

Figure 16

Whenever I draw an odd-shaped diagram, I locate the starting point for the diagram on the diagram page, insert the diagram page into the typewriter, set the starting point in the proper location in the typewriter, and proceed to outline the diagram without any sort of preliminary work.

However, if you have never drawn an odd-shaped diagram—and the chances are that you haven't—perhaps you will find it most practical to start from the very beginning.

For example, if you wish to duplicate the diagram design, as shown in Figure 16, follow the fourteen easy steps, as outlined in the following instructions:

1. Draw a regular 17×17 diagram—properly located on the diagram page.

2. Mark and ink in (with black waterproof India ink) all the outside unused squares in the diagram, as shown in Figure 17.

3. Lay the inked in diagram (Figure 17) face up on a table or desk.

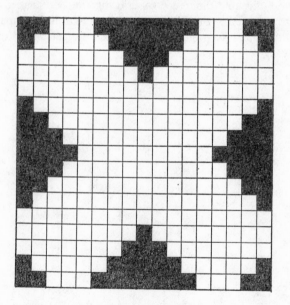

Figure 17

4. Take a clean sheet of typewriter paper and lay it directly over the diagram (Figure 17). (For identification purposes, I call the top

sheet of paper the diagram page.)

5. Square up both sheets of paper so that all four edges are evenly lined up.

6. With a pointed pencil, lightly trace (on the diagram page) the outline of the diagram (Figure 17) where it shows through the diagram page. (Trace only the outline of the white squares in the diagram so that the finished outline on the diagram page is identical with the diagram outline shown in Figure 18.)

7. Place the traced outline (diagram page Figure 18) into the typewriter. Place the starting point of the diagram (Figure 18) in the typewriter carriage just as you would for a regular diagram.

8. Proceed to outline the traced diagram (Figure 18) with dots in the following manner:

(a) Type one dot at the point of each outside corner of the traced diagram outline, as shown by the small arrows in Figure 19, and remember to allow three spaces between the horizontal dots and two spaces between the vertical dots.

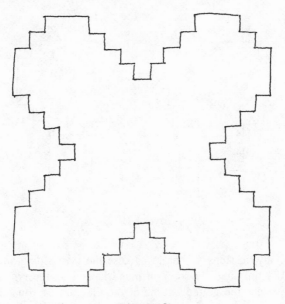

Figure 18

(b) Draw two additional dots (three spaces apart) between all the points marked "A," as shown in Figure 19. Type the two additional

dots between the points marked "A" at the same time that you type
the diagram outline dots at the points of the outside corners—that is,
carry out step (a) and step (b) at the same time.

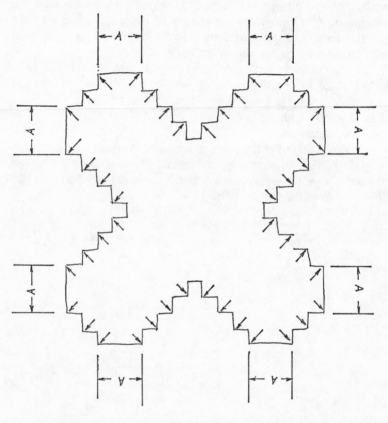

Figure 19

Incidentally, in steps (a) and (b), use the traced diagram outline
(Figure 18) only as a guide. You must depend on the typewriter to
accurately space the dotted outline of the diagram. If you follow the
instructions accurately, then the dotted outline of your diagram will
be identical with the dotted outline of the illustrated diagram as
shown in Figure 20. Notice, too, that the dots in the diagram outline,
as shown in Figure 20, aren't typed at the exact points of the outside

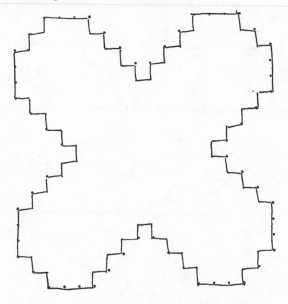

Figure 20

corners of the traced diagram outlines; the dots of the diagram outline seem to be inaccurately spaced. However, don't let that fool you, because the dotted outline of the diagram is accurately spaced— it's the traced diagram outline that is off.

9. Remove the diagram page from the typewriter.

10. Erase the pencil-traced outline of the diagram. Now the dotted outline of your diagram, if it is accurately spaced, will be identical with the dotted diagram outline as shown in Figure 21.

11. Now, with a fountain pen and a steel-edged ruler, draw the vertical lines in the diagram between the horizontal dots, as shown Figure 22.

12. Draw the horizontal lines in the diagram between the vertical dots, as shown in Figure 23.

13. Draw the outside lines, as shown in Figure 24, to complete the diagram.

14. Ink in the 25 unused squares in the diagram, and your finished diagram design will be identical with the diagram design shown in Figure 16. And that's all there is to drawing this type of diagram design.

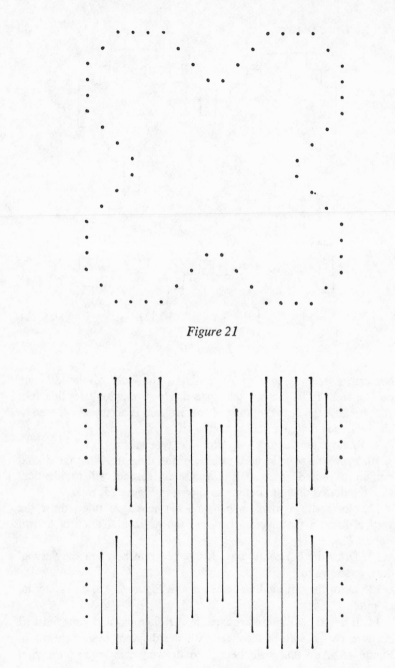

Figure 21

Figure 22

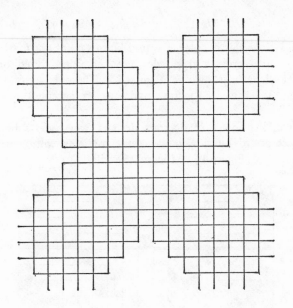

Figure 23

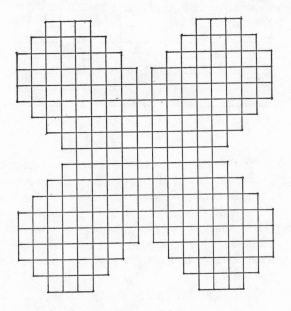

Figure 24

Before I close this chapter, I would like to point out that most of the odd-shaped crossword puzzles are submitted to editors with diagram designs as shown in Figure 25. These types of diagram designs are much easier to draw, and they are accepted by the editors.

However, the choice of diagram designs, when you submit odd-shaped crossword puzzles to an editor, remains with you. Either diagram design (Figure 16 or Figure 25) will do.

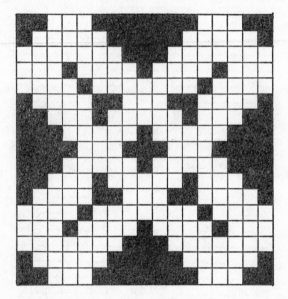

Figure 25

The only noticeable difference between the diagram designs of Figure 16 and Figure 25 is that all the outside unused squares (black squares) have been completely eliminated from the diagram design as shown in Figure 16. Also, this type of diagram design requires a longer period of time to complete, although I must admit, and perhaps you will too, that the diagram design, as shown in Figure 16, presents a much neater-looking diagram page. So—take your choice.

HOW TO FILL IN DIAGRAMS

In Webster's dictionary the crossword puzzle is defined as follows: "A word-guessing puzzle arranged in a diagram in which the words, when correctly supplied, cross each other vertically and horizontally, so that most of the letters appear in two words."

Actually, the foregoing definition explains the diagram section of a crossword puzzle so thoroughly that I don't believe I can add anything of importance to the definition.

To fill in a crossword puzzle diagram with words, you simply select suitable words (or names, occasionally) and try to arrange them—at first, usually through trial and error—in the squares of the diagram to produce a series of words that cross each other in both the horizontal and the vertical positions.

Filling in diagrams doesn't require any kind of special talent. At first, you may find this easy task a bit slow, or perhaps a bit difficult, but in time you will acquire the skill to work rapidly and expertly with words. In fact, anyone who can read, write, and has a normal intelligence can, with a bit of practice, fill in diagrams with the proper kind of words.

But don't expect to become an expert or a professional crossword puzzle constructor over night. I must admit that it does require a certain period of time to become an expert in this field—as with any other field for that matter. This doesn't necessarily mean, however, that you can't construct salable crossword puzzles in a short period of time—of course you can. Just give it a fair trial and really convince yourself that it can be done.

Skill—any kind of skill—is usually acquired over a period of time through practical experience. Some people learn a particular kind of skill much quicker than others. However, with a bit of practice, patience, determination, and, above all, with the complete knowledge of all the important rules and guidelines that you must follow in order to construct salable puzzles, you, too, can become an expert crossword puzzle constructor. And, I might add, in a very much shorter period of time than you might expect.

For your first attempt at filling in a diagram, I suggest that you select a small diagram to practice on—one that contains a large number of three-letter words.

The 13×13 diagram design, as shown in Figure 26, is an excellent one to start with. This particular diagram is designed expressly for practice.

Incidentally, when you actually start to construct crossword puzzles for publication, I suggest that you avoid all diagram designs that are similar to the one in Figure 26. This particular design contains too many three-letter words—a total of thirty-six, to be exact. This

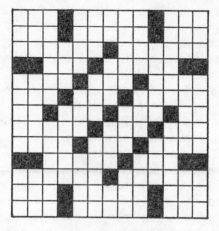

Figure 26

is far too many for a diagram of this size.

Excessive use of two- and three-letter words in a single crossword puzzle—large or small—is undesirable. Practically all three-letter words are considered, by most editors, to be hackneyed words; avoid them whenever you possibly can.

The easiest way to avoid an excessive use of two- and three-letter words in the diagrams is to select diagram designs (from the crossword puzzle magazines) that contain the least number of these kinds of words.

Of course, you will find two- and three-letter words in all sizes of diagram designs. It's practically impossible to eliminate them completely, but, if the two- and three-letter words are kept at a minimum (in the diagram sections of crossword puzzles), the puzzles will be more interesting, and they will stand a much better chance of being accepted for publication by choosy or fussy editors—there are a few of them still around, you know.

Draw about five copies of the diagram design, as shown in Figure 26.

Roughly ink in the unused squares, but do not number the squares in the diagrams—the numbers aren't needed in diagrams that are intended for practice.

Always use a pencil to fill in the rough diagrams. If any mistakes are made—wrong words, misspelled words, duplicate words, etc.— they can be easily erased and corrected.

Don't worry if the three-letter words in the practice diagrams sound hackneyed. What you really should strive for, at this point, is the knack and the ability to fill in the diagrams with words quickly, efficiently, and accurately—with a minimum number of errors and in the shortest period of time.

To fill in a diagram with words, start in the upper left-hand corner of the diagram. Work down and to the right so that you finish filling in the diagram in the lower right-hand corner.

Working from left to right seems to be the most natural and the most practical way to fill in diagrams; however, there will be occasions when you may have to work from right to left in certain sections of the diagrams.

When you start filling in the diagram in the upper left-hand corner, it doesn't make too much difference whether you fill in the longer words first, or whether you fill in the shorter words first. Try it both ways and see which way is the most practical for you.

I generally start with the longer words in the corner, and then I find it much easier to fill in the shorter words, although I must admit that this particular system doesn't work out the same way for me every time. Sometimes I have to start with the shorter words instead of the longer ones.

Actually, I know of no specific rule to follow for filling in diagrams. I believe that every crossword puzzle constructor, through his own experience, must develop his own method for filling in diagrams with the proper words. I merely point out my own method, which I find quite satisfactory for my personal needs. Perhaps you may find it better to experiment with a few different methods and then compare them with one another in order to select the method which you find to be the easiest one to work with.

When you finish filling in the first diagram, lay it aside and start on the next one. I'm sure that you will find, as you proceed with each succeeding diagram, that it becomes much easier to select the proper words to fill in the diagram.

Speed, in this business, is a profitable asset. However, don't fret about it at this point. You will develop it in time.

As you work filling in each diagram, keep in mind the fact that there are many, many words in the English language that can be changed to form a different word and a different meaning merely by changing a single letter.

To illustrate the point, notice how the words in the following examples change to form new and different words merely by changing one letter in each succeeding word. Examples: recent, rebent, redent, regent, relent, repent, rerent, resent; rebend, reband, rebind, remind; recent, decent; resort, retort, report, deport; retort, retore, retire, rewire, rehire, etc.

Observe, for example, as to what happens in the following examples when the first letter of the word "best" is substituted with another suitable letter of the alphabet. Examples: best, jest, lest, nest, pest, vest, west, and zest.

If you wish to insert a new word in the diagram, or if you wish to change only a single letter in a specific word in the diagram, I suggest that you do all this mentally before you use your pencil to see if a new word or a change of a letter in a specific word in the diagram is practical. Ask yourself, for example, will the new word fit? Can a single letter be changed in a specific word? Will the word or the letter change be practical? And, most of all, will it serve the purpose for which the change is intended?

I suggest that you get in the habit of using your brain before using your pencil. You will find that this method, when properly used, will save an enormous amount of unnecessary erasing. It's much easier and, I might add, much quicker to erase an unsuitable word or a letter from your mind than from your diagram.

For a bit of mental exercise, see how many legitimate four-letter words you can form by filling in the missing letters in the following three examples. However, before you start this exercise, I would like to point out that the easiest way to find and form legitimate words in the following examples, is to start with the letter "A"—do it mentally, of course—and go through the entire alphabet one letter at a time. When you find a suitable letter of the alphabet that forms a legitimate word, write it down. It's that simple.

Example 1: BAL_

(In this example, you should be able to form at least 6 legitimate words.)

Example 2: B_L_

(Use the same method for this example. You should be able to form at least 20 legitimate words.)

Example 3: _ _LL

(In this example, if you use the same method, you should be able to form at least 45 legitimate words.)

Or you might try a few of your own examples. I'm sure you will find this kind of exercise beneficial and stimulating.

For additional fill-in exercises, draw several copies of the diagram design shown in Figure 27. This particular diagram was also de-

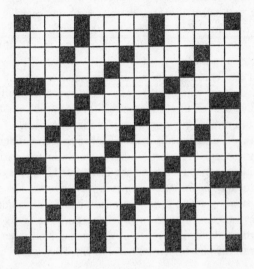

Figure 27

signed for practice use only. It contains a large number of two-, three-, and four-letter words; therefore, it's an ideal diagram design to practice on. It contains ten designated spaces for two-letter words —about six too many for a diagram of this size. It will, however, give you an ideal opportunity to use a few abbreviations, chemical symbols, etc., in the two-letter spaces.

When you feel you've made some progress in filling in diagrams, select a few diagrams (from any crossword puzzle magazine) that are designed to accept five- and six-letter words, and see if you can fill them in. Take your time with these diagram designs. Don't work for speed—at least not at this point.

In time, you will learn through experience, as I did, that most diagrams that are designed to accept a large number of three- and four-letter words are rather easy to fill in.

Diagrams designed to accept a large number of five-letter words that cross each other (especially in the corners) are somewhat difficult to fill in.

And diagrams designed to accept a large number of six-letter words that cross each other in the corners, or in any other sections of the diagrams, are very difficult to fill in. Try them if you wish to get some practice; otherwise, avoid them whenever you possibly can. Whenever you select diagram designs for your puzzles, always keep in mind the fact that the longer the words in the diagrams—especially when they cross each other—the more difficult the diagrams become to fill in.

Most of the better diagrams are designed to accept a few of the longer words, and you shouldn't have too much difficulty filling them in. In fact, a few of the longer words are desirable in the diagrams; however, too many long words usually mean trouble.

For my own crossword puzzles, I always select diagrams that are designed to accept four- or five-letter words in the corners. I would like to point out that I do have the ability to fill in diagrams that are designed to accept six-letter words in the corners. In fact, I did it many times when I was a beginner in this field and didn't know any better. The fact remains, however, that regardless of the time I spend filling in these particular types of diagrams, I still receive only the standard rate of pay for these puzzles. So, why waste extra time for nothing?

At the beginning, you may find it somewhat difficult to distinguish the good diagram designs from the bad ones. However, with a bit of practice—especially after you get stuck with a few bad diagram designs—you will learn how to select good diagram designs for your puzzles. You will know at a glance which diagram designs to select and which to reject.

When you select sample diagram designs for your crossword puzzles, besides being careful to select diagrams that are designed to accept four- or five-letter words in the corners, there is one more specific point you should look for—the direction in which the diagonal rows of black squares run. In most diagram designs, the diagonal rows of black squares usually run from right to left, as shown in Figure 28, but in others, the diagonal rows of black squares run from left to right, as shown in Figure 29.

Generally you will find, as I did through practical experience, that diagram designs shown in Figure 28 are much easier to fill in than the diagram designs shown in Figure 29. But, of course, you don't have to take my word for it. Try filling in a few diagram designs as shown in Figure 29 if you really want to be convinced. Perhaps you

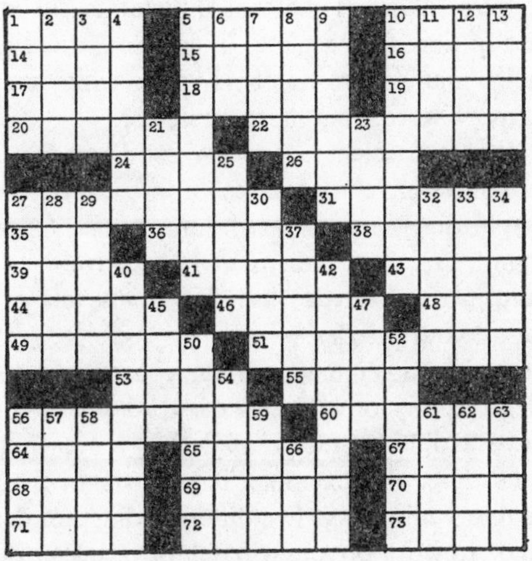

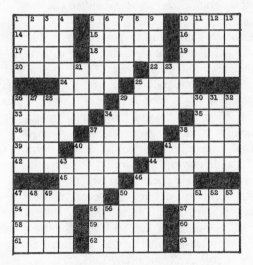

Figure 28

Figure 29

may be lucky with one or two diagrams—depending of course on the sizes of the diagrams—and have no difficulty filling them in. But as a rule you will find that practically all the diagrams similar to the one shown in Figure 29 are somewhat difficult to fill in and require a longer period of time to complete. In addition, these types of diagram designs require many more numbers in the white squares of the diagrams—not more words, but more numbers.

I suggest that you select about ten good sample diagram designs (from crossword puzzle magazines) for each different puzzle size. Cut the sample diagrams out of the magazines (together with their definition numbers), insert them in large envelopes, and put them aside for future use. You can use these same diagram designs over and over for all your puzzles.

The main point to remember when you submit a batch of crossword puzzles (or any other types of word puzzles) to an editor is that you have a different diagram design for each puzzle that you submit at one time. For example, if you submit five puzzles of one specific size to an editor, use five different diagram designs. And then when you start to work on a new batch of puzzles, use the same sample diagrams for your new puzzles. After all, no editor who receives hundreds of different word puzzles each month is going to remember the kind of diagram designs you submitted the previous week or the previous month.

The point that I'm trying to put across is this: Select a specific number of good diagram designs and stick with them—use the same diagram designs for all your puzzles. Of course, if you wish to select a large variety of sample diagrams, you may do so. However, when you get used to filling in specific types of diagrams, you will have less difficulty in finding suitable words for the diagrams.

Occasionally, when you work filling in a diagram, you may find that you can't proceed any farther in a certain section of the diagram for lack of a suitable word (or words) for a specific space. Whenever a situation such as this occurs, don't become discouraged. This kind of situation occurs quite frequently even to the experienced crossword puzzle constructors. The solution is a simple one. Whenever you get stuck in a diagram, erase a few of the last words that you entered in the diagram and start a new course of action with different words. If you still can't make any noticeable progress, erase a few additional words in the diagram and try it again.

If you are working on a small-size diagram and you run into a snag, perhaps you will be better off if you erase all the words in the diagram and start again from the beginning.

On the other hand, if the diagram on which you are working is one of the larger sizes and you can't make any kind of progress filling it in for lack of a suitable word (or words), lay the diagram aside for the time being and start to work on another diagram—that is, if you are working on more than one puzzle.

Many times when you get stuck in a diagram, anxiety develops a mental block so that you can't think properly. Whenever you get yourself into this kind of a predicament, relax. There is no need to get irritated over a crossword puzzle. If you can't complete a diagram in the same day, try it again the next day, or the day after. Usually there is a solution to this kind of problem, and you will find it if you just take your time.

After you gain a bit of experience with the smaller puzzles, don't be afraid to experiment with the larger ones. Remember, if you have the ability to construct the small-size puzzles, you also have the ability to construct the larger ones. The only extra requirement you will need to construct the larger size puzzles is confidence. The noticeable difference between constructing the larger puzzle as opposed to the smaller puzzle is the time element; the larger ones require a longer period of time to complete.

Before I close this chapter, I would like to suggest that if you have any kind of difficulty getting your crossword puzzle diagrams started, turn to the answer pages of any crossword puzzle magazine, and you will find a selection of many suitable words. So don't worry too much about this problem. In time you will develop your own method for getting your diagrams started.

HOW TO TYPE THE NUMBERS AND THE WORDS IN THE DIAGRAMS

In the finished diagrams (the diagrams that are submitted to the editors), all the numbers and all the words (in capitals) *must* be typed in the diagrams with a typewriter. However, don't let this statement frighten you. If you follow the detailed instructions presented in this chapter, you will find that this particular operation is not really as difficult to carry out as you might imagine.

I can assure you that it's quite easy to type the numbers and the words in the finished diagrams. And with a bit of practice, you will find that you, too, can carry out this operation quickly and efficiently.

The most important step in this particular operation is to learn how to position the first square of the diagram (on the diagram page) quickly and correctly in the typewriter so that when you strike the number 1 key on the typewriter keyboard, the 1 will appear in the upper left-hand corner of the first square in the diagram, as shown in Figure 30-a.

If the first number (1) is typed correctly in the first square of the diagram, all the following numbers and words will fall automatically into their proper places. It's that simple. On the other hand, if the first number (1) is typed incorrectly in the first square of the diagram, all the following numbers and words will be typed incorrectly in all the individual squares throughout the entire diagram.

To illustrate a point, observe the illustrated examples, as shown in Figure 30-a, b, c, d, e, and f.

In the first example (Figure 30-a), the number 1 is typed correctly in the first square of the diagram. Notice how all the following numbers and words line up properly in all the individual squares of this diagram. Even if this were a large 23×23 diagram, all the numbers and words would still line up properly.

In the second example (Figure 30-b), you will notice that the number 1 is typed a bit farther to the right in the first square of the diagram. Notice, too, that all the following numbers and words are typed slightly to the right in all the squares of the diagram. Notice, in this particular example, that even though all the numbers and words are typed slightly to the right in the individual squares, they all still line up properly.

In the third example (Figure 30-c), the first two-digit number (10) in the first square of the diagram is typed too low and too far to the right. Notice that all the following numbers and words in the individual squares of the diagram are typed too low and too far to the right.

In the fourth example (Figure 30-d), the first three-digit number (100) is typed too far to the right in the first square. In fact, this number is typed so far to the right that the last digit of this number spills over into the adjoining square. Notice, in this example, that all the last digits of the following numbers also spill over into the adjoining squares. However, pay particular attention to the words in this diagram—all the letters of each word line up perfectly in the center of each individual square. The reason for this is that I readjusted the diagram just before I typed in the words. So keep in mind the fact that you can readjust the diagram at any point of this operation to correct a number or a letter of a word that is out of line.

However, before you begin to worry too much about typing in the

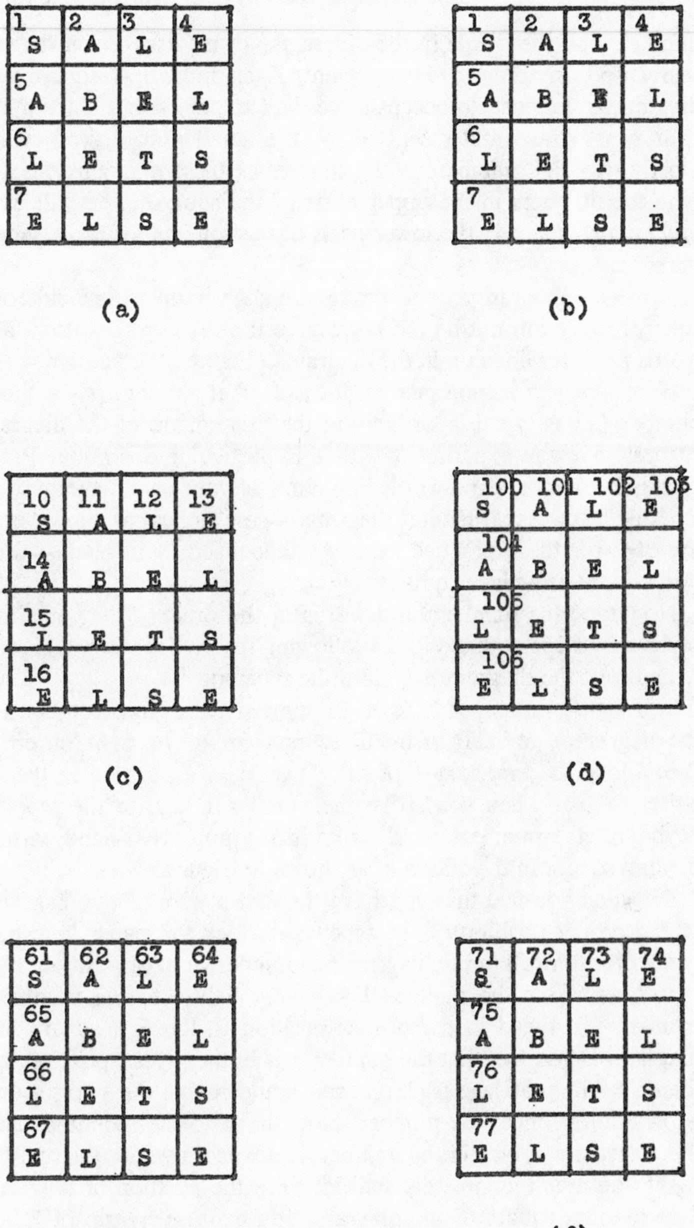

1 S	2 A	3 L	4 E
5 A	B	E	L
6 L	E	T	S
7 E	L	S	E

(a)

1 S	2 A	3 L	4 E
5 A	B	E	L
6 L	E	T	S
7 E	L	S	E

(b)

10 S	11 A	12 L	13 E
14 A	B	E	L
15 L	E	T	S
16 E	L	S	E

(c)

100 S	101 A	102 L	103 E
104 A	B	E	L
105 L	E	T	S
106 E	L	S	E

(d)

61 S	62 A	63 L	64 E
65 A	B	E	L
66 L	E	T	S
67 E	L	S	E

(e)

71 S	72 A	73 L	74 E
75 A	B	E	L
76 L	E	T	S
77 E	L	S	E

(f)

Figure 30

numbers and the words in the diagrams, let me assure you that there really isn't anything to worry about. Each individual square in the diagram is designed to accept three-digit numbers, but since most of your crossword puzzles will be of the smaller sizes, you will use mostly two-digit numbers in the squares of these diagrams. So if you type the numbers in the upper parts of the squares, you will usually find enough space in the lower parts of the squares for the letters that make up the words.

If the numbers in your diagrams are slightly off to one side of the squares, they will not be too noticeable if you keep the letters of the words properly lined up in the diagrams (Figure 30-e and f).

Now that you have a general idea of what happens when the first number (1) is typed incorrectly in the first square of the diagram, I suggest that you experiment with this particular operation. Practice typing the numbers and words into a few of your own diagrams.

Draw a few experimental diagrams—small ones, as shown in Figure 30—for these practice exercises, and keep them blank—that is, don't ink in any black squares.

Now type the numbers and words in the practice diagrams in the seven easy steps outlined in the following instructions:

1. Insert the diagram page into the typewriter.

2. Release the paper lock on the typewriter so that you can move the diagram page freely in any direction—up, down, right, or left.

3. Move the first square of the diagram to a position in the typewriter so that when you strike the number 1 key on the typewriter keyboard, the number 1 will strike in the upper left-hand corner of the first square in the diagram, as shown in Figure 30-a.

4. When you feel that you have the first square of the diagram set in the proper position of the typewriter, lock the paper lock on the typewriter to prevent the diagram from moving out of position.

5. Now strike the number 1 key very lightly to see whether the number 1 is typed in the proper position in the first square of the diagram. If you feel that the number 1 is in the proper position, move the typewriter carriage back one space and retype the 1 to produce a good impression of the number. Now move to the second square of the diagram and type in the number 2, etc. as shown in Figure 30-a.

(If you aren't completely satisfied with the position of the number 1 in the first square of the diagram, you can use a strip of Ko-Rec-Type to strike out the impression. Then you can readjust the first square of the diagram in the typewriter and try it again. Or you can readjust the second square of the diagram for the number 2 and go on from there.)

6. After you have the four numbers typed in the first row of squares, move the typewriter carriage back to the number 1 position. Now drop down one space and move one space to the right.

7. Now type in the four letters (in capitals) that make up the first word—type one letter into each individual square, and keep in mind the fact that there are three spaces between each letter.

When you practice typing in the numbers and the words in your practice diagrams, I suggest that you remove the diagram page completely from the typewriter after you type in the numbers and the words in each individual row of squares. And then reinsert the diagram page in the typewriter, properly adjust the first square in the second row of squares (Figure 30-a, ⚡5), and repeat the seven steps to complete the second row of squares in the diagram, etc.

The main reason for removing the diagram page from the typewriter after typing in the numbers and the words in each individual row of squares is that this extra step will give you additional practice in positioning the first square of the diagram properly in the typewriter quickly and accurately on the very first attempt.

If you're not completely satisfied with the results of your first attempt in typing the numbers and the words in the practice diagrams, I suggest that you draw a few extra practice diagrams, and try it again.

The main point of the instructions in this particular section boils down to one important fact: Type the number 1 correctly in the proper position in the first square of the diagram and all the following numbers and words will fall into their proper places in the squares automatically. It's that simple. And remember, too, that you can readjust the diagram at any point of the operation when you're typing in the numbers or the words in the diagram.

Before I close this section, I would like to point out that when the numbers and the words are typed in the finished stage of the diagram page, all the numbers are typed in the diagram first. Then the diagram page is rolled back to the number 1 position in the first square, and all the words are typed in the diagram. So you see if the numbers in your diagram are slightly off to one side, you can always readjust the diagram page to correct the position of the words in the diagram. I believe that most editors of crossword puzzle magazines are more concerned with the alignment of the words in the diagram rather than the numbers, because when all the words line up properly, they are easy to read and can be checked quickly without any eyestrain.

HOW TO DRAW AND PREPARE THE DIAGRAM PAGE

The diagram page is the sheet of paper on which you draw the crossword puzzle diagram—or any other type of word puzzle diagram.

In practically all the requirement sheets for crossword puzzles, you will find that the instructions for preparing the diagram pages are alike.

The diagram, all editors agree, must be drawn with black ink on a separate sheet of standard 8½ × 11 white bond paper. It must be symmetrical (square) with all the white squares keyed to one another. The squares in the diagram must be large enough so that the numbers and the words (in capitals) can be typed in and easily read. It must be a combination diagram and answer box with all the black squares (unused squares) inked in solid.

In the upper right-hand corner of the diagram page, type your name, your address, and the source of reference—the name of the dictionary from which you have selected the words for your diagram and their definitions.

1 P	2 I	3 T	4 C	5 H	■	6 S	7 L	8 A	9 B	■	10 P	11 A	12 S	13 T
14 A	N	I	L	E	■	15 T	I	T	O	■	16 A	L	T	O
17 S	T	E	E	R	■	18 E	V	E	R	■	19 R	E	A	P
20 S	O	D	A	■	21 A	V	E	■	22 R	23 I	C	E	R	S
■	■	24 N	25 I	C	E	■	26 B	O	R	E	■	■	■	■
27 R	28 E	29 V	E	R	E	■	30 B	E	W	I	L	31 D	32 E	33 R
34 A	R	I	S	E	■	35 R	O	L	E	S	■	36 A	R	E
37 T	A	C	T	■	38 S	E	N	O	R	■	39 S	N	O	W
40 E	T	A	■	41 S	T	R	E	W	■	42 S	W	E	D	E
43 S	O	R	44 E	H	E	A	D	■	45 P	O	I	S	E	D
■	■	46 R	O	A	N	■	47 T	O	W	N	■	■	■	■
48 B	49 A	50 R	R	E	L	■	51 H	A	D	■	52 D	53 R	54 I	55 P
56 O	L	I	O	■	57 E	58 V	I	L	■	59 E	L	I	D	E
60 M	O	O	R	■	61 R	I	D	E	■	62 R	E	L	E	T
63 B	E	T	S	■	64 S	E	E	S	■	65 A	R	E	A	S

Figure 31

Most editors of crossword puzzle magazines clearly specify that your name, address, and the source of reference must be typed in the upper right-hand corner of the diagram page. However, this practice isn't a set rule. So don't be surprised if some editor instructs you to type the same information in the upper left-hand corner of the diagram page.

In addition to your name, address, and the source of reference, some editors may also require a word count—the number of words that appear in the diagram section of your crossword puzzle. The word count is usually entered on the diagram page directly beneath the source of reference.

Some editors may even go one step farther in their requirements. They may request that the puzzle size also be included with the other information on the diagram page. If the puzzle size must be included, type it directly beneath the word count on the diagram page.

HOW TO SELECT AND USE GOOD DEFINITIONS

A definition is simply an explanation of what a particular word or phrase means.

You must give a definition for each word in the crossword puzzle diagram. A good definition is usually well-arranged, clear, concise, and appropriately expressed. It must be accurate, and it must quickly identify the called-for word.

For easy definitions, I suggest that you use common definitions, and limit them to two or three words if you possibly can—make them short and to the point. Easy, clear, and concise definitions will not only help the puzzle solver to solve your puzzles more rapidly but will also help to sell more of your puzzles to the editors of puzzle magazines.

Many words have different meanings. Always select the definition that carries the easiest meaning. Don't define hard words—or easy words, for that matter—with harder definitions. Keep the definitions simple, unless the publication to which you intend to submit your puzzles uses difficult or sophisticated definitions.

Avoid the use of far-fetched, complex, unusually long, or difficult and uninteresting definitions. Short, easy definitions—common definitions which everyone is familiar with—are most suitable for crossword puzzles.

When a specific word carries a difficult or complex definition, I suggest that you pass it up unless you can find a simple synonym to use as a definition.

By all means avoid definitions that are similar to the definitions illustrated in the following examples—long, difficult, complicated, and uninteresting. (These specific definitions, I'm happy to say, were constructed deliberately to show a few exaggerated examples of the type of definitions you must avoid in your puzzles. I must admit, however, that many definitions such as the following examples do appear occasionally in crossword puzzles.)

1. Path of the sun as Daniel Boone saw it   WEST
2. Unit of measure used by bakers   DOZEN
3. English editor, chronicler, and antiquary (1525–1605)   STOW
4. On the left-hand side of a wagon   NIGH
5. What a frightened cat does to its back   ARCH
6. Something not mixed or compounded   SIMPLE
7. Case holding the main spring of a watch or clock   BARREL
8. Direction in which Marco Polo traveled   EAST
9. To keep cool, this garment should not be worn in July   OVER-COAT
10. What the nightingale did in Barkley Square   SANG

When you compare the answer words with their definitions in the preceding examples, you can readily see that the definitions are too long, too difficult, and too complicated for the simple answer words. Shorter and easier definitions (common definitions), as shown in the following examples are more suitable for the simple answer words.

1. Direction of sunset   WEST
2. 12 eggs   DOZEN
3. Store away   STOW
4. Almost   NIGH
5. Archway   ARCH
6. Easy to do   SIMPLE
7. Large bulging cask   BARREL
8. Direction of sunrise   EAST
9. Topcoat   OVERCOAT
10. Vocalized   SANG

Practically all crossword puzzle constructors, at one time or another, use the names of prominent people in their crossword puzzle diagrams. Some editors may frown upon this practice. However, the majority of them have no objections to using names in the diagram sections—provided, of course, that there aren't too many names in one puzzle.

Whenever you use a name (or names) of a prominent person in the diagram section of a crossword puzzle, always try to compose the definition (for a specific name) in a manner that will identify the called-for name quickly. This can be done quite easily if you associate the person's name with his profession, as shown in the following examples:

1. Pro golfer   PALMER
2. Baseballer Berra   YOGI
3. Heavyweight champion CLAY

You can also apply this same method to many of the common English given names, such as Helen, Ann, Rita, James, Glenn, etc.

It's much easier to identify a given name quickly when you associate the name with a well-known personality or a profession. This method practically eliminates all the guesswork from the definitions.

In most of the crossword puzzle definitions, you will find that the given names are usually defined in three different ways, as shown in the following examples: (Note how the following definitions identify the given names easily and quickly without any fuss or bother.)

1. Miss Hayworth   RITA
2. Miss Horne   LENA
3. Mr. Ford   GLENN

1. Miss Hayworth, actress   RITA
2. Miss Horne, songstress   LENA
3. Mr. Ford, actor   GLENN

1. Actress — Hayworth   RITA
2. Songstress — Horne   LENA
3. Actor — Ford   GLENN

Among the many different types of definitions, there is one type of definition that is known as the missing-word definition. This particular type of definition is self-explanatory; it's simply an ordinary definition with a missing word. In fact, the definitions in the above ⊁3 examples are really missing-word definitions. Definitions of this type are used quite frequently by practically all the crossword puzzle constructors.

Usually you will find that the missing-word definitions are used to define two- or three-word names, such as alma mater, Notre Dame, Iwo Jima, Ali Baba, Des Moines, Las Vegas, Ponce de Leon, Rio de Janeiro, Grand Coulee Dam, etc., as shown in the following examples:

1.	— Jima	IWO
2.	Iwo —	JIMA
3.	Notre —	DAME
4.	— Dame	NOTRE
5.	Ponce de —	LEON
6.	Ponce — Leon	DE
7.	— de Leon	PONCE

Missing-word definitions are also used to define two- or three-word phrases when one word of the phrase is missing, as shown in the following examples:

1.	Snick and —	SNEE
2.	— and snee	SNICK
3.	Up — down	OR
4.	Up or —	DOWN
5.	Sink or —	SWIM
6.	— or swim	SINK

Besides being used to define two- or three-word names and phrases, missing-word definitions are also used quite frequently to define single words, as shown in the following examples:

1.	Apple —	PIE
2.	The sky is —	BLUE
3.	Safety —	PIN
4.	Roses are —	RED

Missing-word definitions are quite popular with most beginners in this field. Whenever they can't find a suitable definition for a particular word, they usually turn to the missing-word definition. This, of course, is one way of getting out of a troublesome spot; however, this practice should not be overdone. The fact is that there are very few suitable words in the English language that can't be satisfactorily defined in crossword puzzle definitions.

Keep in mind the fact that there are some editors who allow only a few, if any, missing-word definitions. I suggest that you be guided by the information in the editors' requirement sheets or by the number of missing-word definitions that are used in their puzzle magazines.

Whenever an occasion occurs that you can't find a suitable definition for a simple word (or difficult word, for that matter), try the opposite-word definition—that is, use a word in the definition whose meaning is opposite to that of the answer word, as shown in the following examples:

1. Opposite of thinnest   FATTEST
2. Opposite of darkest   LIGHTEST
3. Opposite of shortest   LONGEST
4. Opposite of up   DOWN
5. Opposite of downward   UPWARD

This type of definition, as shown in the preceding examples, is also ideal for short words in the diagram that require long or complicated definitions. However, again let me warn you—don't overdo it.

Never start definitions with articles (a, an, the) or with prepositions (at, to, in, etc.), as shown in the following examples, unless the definition calls for an article or a preposition to clarify it.

1. A spirited horse   STEED
2. A kind of fruit   APPLE
3. An ocean   SEA
4. To immerse in dye   DIP
5. The 13th letter   EM

Definitions, such as the ones shown in the preceding examples, really show the trade-mark of an amateur. Eliminate the articles and the prepositions from the definitions, as shown in the following examples:

1. Spirited horse   STEED
2. Kind of fruit   APPLE
3. Ocean   SEA
4. Immerse in dye   DIP
5. 13th letter   EM

The prepositions at the beginning of the following definitions are permissable in order to clarify their meanings.

1. To the time of   UNTIL
2. At home   IN
3. In opposition to   AGAINST
4. To be added   ADDITIVE
5. In that manner   SO

Without the prepositions, the preceding definition examples are incomplete and misleading, as you will notice in the following examples:

1. The time of   UNTIL
2. Home   IN
3. Opposition to   AGAINST
4. Be added   ADDITIVE
5. That manner   SO

Many key words, such as tool, appliance, instrument, implement, ingredient, utensil, derivative, receptacle, measure, part, beverage, garment, land measure, dry measure, liquid measure, distance measure, vehicle, etc. are used quite frequently in definitions. Keep a complete list of them handy.

Many simple words carry difficult and/or long definitions. Many such definitions can be shortened simply by using certain key words in the definitions, as shown in the following examples:

1. Carpenter's tool   HAMMER
2. Sewing implement   NEEDLE
3. Measuring instrument   METER
4. Candy ingredient   SUGAR
5. Sugar derivative   MOLASSES
6. Flower receptacle   VASE
7. Malt beverage   ALE
8. Distance measure   MILE
9. Land measure   ACRE
10. Snow vehicle   SLED

HOW TO USE TENSES IN THE DEFINITIONS

In reference to the definitions, another important bit of information that you must remember is the fact that the tenses of the definitions must match the tenses of the answer words, as shown in the following examples:

1. Waltz   (present tense)   DANCE   (present tense)
2. Stroll   (present tense)   WALK   (present tense)
3. Sing   (present tense)   CROON   (present tense)

Now observe the same words and the same definitions in the past tense, as shown in the following examples:

1. Waltzed   (past tense)   DANCED   (past tense)
2. Strolled   (past tense)   WALKED   (past tense)
3. Sang   (past tense)   CROONED   (past tense)

Words that end with the suffix "ing" are in the present tense. Whenever you use words that end with the suffix "ing" in the diagram section of a puzzle, be sure that the tenses of the definitions match the tenses of the answer words, as shown in the following examples:

1. Waltz(ing)   DANC(ING)
2. Stroll(ing)   WALK(ING)
3. Sing(ing)   CROON(ING)

HOW TO INDICATE PLURALS IN DEFINITIONS

Whenever you use a plural word in the diagram section of a crossword puzzle, the definition for it must indicate to the puzzle solver that the word is in the plural form.

Some requirement sheets for crossword puzzles illustrate with examples the manner in which the editors wish to indicate plural form definitions on the definition pages. Many requirement sheets, however, give no instructions on this subject. When this is the case, simply look through the publisher's puzzle magazines to see what method he uses.

To indicate plural form definitions, there are only three methods most publishers use in their crossword puzzle magazines. In the first method, this is shown simply by printing the abbreviation of the word plural (pl.) in parentheses directly after the definition, as shown in the following examples:

1. Kind of fruit (pl.)   APPLES
2. Citrus fruit (pl.)   LEMONS
3. Red-breasted bird (pl.) ROBINS

In the second method, the definition carries the abbreviation "pl." directly after a colon which follows the definitions, as shown in the following examples:

1. Kind of fruit: pl.   APPLES
2. Citrus fruit: pl.   LEMONS
3. Red-breasted bird: pl.   ROBINS

In the third method, and you will find this to be true in many crossword puzzle magazines, the editors simply eliminate the abbreviation of the word plural and add "s" or "es" to their definitions, as shown in the following examples:

1. Kinds of fruits   APPLES
2. Citrus fruits   LEMONS
3. Red-breasted birds   ROBINS

About the only thing that you need to remember about the indication of plural form definitions is the fact that whenever you submit any crossword puzzles (or any other types of word puzzles) make it a rule to use the same method the publisher uses in his crossword puzzle magazines. If you stick to this rule, you will have no difficulty with the indication of plural forms in your definitions.

STYLE AND SETUP

Style and setup in the printing field simply means the general make-up of a publication—size, shape, printing style, form, usage, etc. However, the only part of this information that really concerns you —the puzzle constructor—at this time is the indication of form (comp. wd., 2 wds., comb. form, etc.) and usage (slang, colloq., pre., French, etc.).

Many editors include this information on form and usage in their requirement sheets for crossword puzzles. However, there are many editors who completely omit this important bit of information from their requirement sheets so that you must acquire this information by studying their crossword puzzle magazines.

If this bit of information seems trivial to you, let me assure you that it can mean the difference between your puzzles being accepted or rejected. The construction of the crossword puzzles you submit to an editor must conform to the style that is used in the magazines he edits.

Generally you will find that the indication of form and usage is presented in most crossword puzzle magazines by one of two methods.

In the first method, the indication of form and usage follows a colon after the definition, as shown in the following examples:

1. On the sea: comp. wd.   ASEA
2. Public storehouse: French   ETAPE
3. Boon companion: slang   PAL

In the second method, the indication of form and usage also follows a definition. However in this method, the indication is enclosed in parentheses and the colon is omitted, as shown in the following examples:

1. On the sea (comp. wd.)   ASEA
2. Public storehouse (French)   ETAPE
3. Boon companion (slang)   PAL

Occasionally you may use a word (or words) in the diagram section of your puzzle that requires comments of both form and usage after the definition. Whenever an occasion such as this occurs, conform to the publisher's style and present them in exactly the same manner as they are presented in his magazines. You will find that the form and usage comments, when used together in a single definition, are usually presented in one of three methods, as shown in the following examples:

1. Very tired (2 wds. colloq.)   ALL IN
2. Very tired: 2 wds. colloq.   ALL IN
3. Very tired: 2 wds. (colloq.)   ALL IN

In all crossword puzzle magazines the following list of words is generally used in the abbreviated form:

Abbreviation, Abbr., abbr., ab.; Latin, Lat., L.; colloquial, Colloq., colloq., coll.; 2 words, 2 wds.; slang, sl.; combining form, comb. form; prefix, pre.; suffix, suf., suff.; dialect, dial.; obsolete, obs.; archaic, arch.; musical, mus.; Scotch, Scot.; poetic, poet., etc.

Names of countries, such as France, Germany, Spain, England, etc., or adjectives pertaining to countries, such as French, German, Spanish, English, etc., may or may not be abbreviated. It all depends, of course, on the publisher's style. If this bit of information isn't included in the publisher's requirement sheet, then you must check through his magazines.

I would like to add one last bit of advice on this subject: Conform to the publisher's style for all word puzzles and you will have a minimum of difficulty.

HOW TO PREPARE THE DEFINITION PAGES

The definition pages are the pages on which you type the definitions for the answer words in the diagram section of the crossword puzzle.

You will find—as you study different requirement sheets for crossword puzzles—that practically all the editors of crossword puzzle magazines have their own particular ideas on the manner in which the definitions must be typed on the definition pages. Because the rules and the general instructions vary in different requirement sheets, I will give you a general idea of how the different definition pages are prepared. In addition, I will explain some of the different methods used by various editors to prepare (type) the definition pages.

The definitions and usually the answer words (in capitals) must be typed on separate sheets of standard 8½ × 11 white bond paper. The definitions must be double-spaced on the definition pages, and usually—but not always—the definitions are listed two columns to one definition page. The columns of definitions must be kept straight with ample margins on all four sides of the definition pages— depending, of course, on the length of the definitions. At the top of the first column of the definition pages, type the word ACROSS or DOWN (in capitals), as the case may be. And for that professional look, the definition pages should be kept clean and uniform throughout.

In the upper right-hand corner of each definition page (unless you are instructed to do otherwise) type your name and address in accordance with the instructions in the requirement sheets for cross-word puzzles, as shown in the following example.

John Doe, Jr.
1635 Woodland Rd.
Cannon, Va. 11776

(And some editors may instruct you to type this same material in the upper left-hand corner of each definition page.)

Or you may be instructed to type only your name in the upper right-hand corner of each definition page.

Another instruction might be to type only your name at the top and center of the first definition page, as shown in the following example.

by
John Doe, Jr.

As you study the different requirement sheets for crossword puzzles, you may be somewhat surprised to find that practically all the editors have their own specific rules and guidelines on the manner in which the definitions must be typed on the definition pages.

For example, some editors may instruct you to type the definition numbers first, the periods second, the definitions third, and the answer words last, as shown in the following example.

1. Antlered animal   DEER

Some editors may instruct you to omit the periods after the definition numbers, as shown in the following example.

1 Antlered animal   DEER

And some editors may instruct you to type only the definition numbers, the periods, and the definitions (omit the answer words), as shown in the following example.

1. Antlered animal

And then, some editors may instruct you to type the answer words first, the definition numbers second, the periods third, and the definitions last, as shown in the following example.

DEER   1. Antlered animal

Some editors may even instruct you to type the definitions in single columns on the definition pages—one column of definitions to each definition page—with 1½″ margins on the sides of the definition pages, as shown in the following example.

1. Antlered animal

Now perhaps you can clearly see the reason that the requirement sheets for all types of word puzzles are so very important to the constructors.

The most practical bit of advice I can offer to the beginner on this subject is: Study the editor's requirement sheets for crossword puzzles thoroughly, and prepare your definition pages according to those instructions. Study the examples in this section and the illustrated examples in Figures 32 and 33. With these examples to guide you plus the instructions on the requirement sheets, I'm sure you'll have no difficulty in preparing the definition pages properly so that they meet the requirements of the individual editors.

HOW TO PREPARE AND USE THE PROOF SHEET

The proof sheet is a specially prepared sheet of paper that has been divided into a series of small sections. Each individual section is designated by a letter of the alphabet for easy location. The proof sheet is used mainly as a means for double-checking all the words in the diagram section for duplicate words.

The proof sheet is another one of my own inventions which I have developed and perfected over a period of time. It is quite simple to prepare and use.

As a beginner, when you start to fill in the crossword puzzle diagrams with words, you probably will discover, as I did, that you are faced with two minor problems, which occur quite frequently and

John Doe, Jr.
1635 Woodland Rd.
Cannon, Va. 11776

ACROSS

1.	Throw	PITCH	40.	Greek letter	ETA
6.	Thick slice	SLAB	41.	Spread by scattering	STREW
10.	Just gone by	PAST	42.	Native of Sweden	SWEDE
14.	Old-womanish	ANILE	43.	Disgruntled person (colloq.)	SOREHEAD
15.	Yugoslavian president	TITO	45.	Balanced or suspended	POISED
16.	Singing voice	ALTO	46.	Bay horse	ROAN
17.	Guide	STEER	47.	Small city	TOWN
18.	Always	EVER	48.	Large bulging cask	BARREL
19.	Harvest	REAP	51.	Possessed	HAD
20.	Ice cream ────	SODA	52.	Fall in drops	DRIP
21.	───Maria	AVE	56.	Medley	OLIO
22.	Kitchen utensils	RICERS	57.	Wicked	EVIL
24.	Fastidious	NICE	59.	Annul	ELIDE
26.	Drill	BORE	60.	Anchor a ship	MOOR
27.	Venerate	REVERE	61.	Go by car	RIDE
30.	Puzzle	BEWILDER	62.	Rerent	RELET
34.	Ascend	ARISE	63.	Wagers	BETS
35.	Actor's parts	ROLES	64.	Observes	SEES
36.	Exist	ARE	65.	Regions	AREAS
37.	Poise	TACT			
38.	Mister (Sp.)	SENOR			
39.	Winter flakes	SNOW			

Figure 32

John Doe, Jr.
1635 Woodland Rd.
Cannon, Va. 11776

DOWN

1.	Term in football	PASS	30.	Removed the bones from	BONED
2.	Toward the inside	INTO	31.	Natives of Denmark	DANES
3.	Bound with string	TIED	32.	Wear away	ERODE
4.	Purest	CLEANEST	33.	Remarry	REWED
5.	That girl	HER	35.	Ran again	RERAN
6.	Steven's nickname	STEVE	38.	Thieves	STEALERS
7.	Reside	LIVE	39.	Cheater	SWINDLER
8.	Consumed food	ATE	41.	Slipper or pump	SHOE
9.	Opposite of lender	BORROWER	42.	Scatter seed	SOW
10.	Package	PARCEL	44.	Mistakes	ERRORS
11.	Toward the lee	ALEE	45.	Seed container	POD
12.	Asterisk	STAR	47.	Fairy stories	TALES
13.	Spinning toys	TOPS	48.	Atom -----	BOMB
21.	High card	ACE	49.	Drug plant	ALOE
23.	Spring flower	IRIS	50.	Tumult	RIOT
25.	Anger	IRE	51.	Conceal	HIDE
26.	Beneath	BELOW	53.	Irritate (colloq.)	RILE
27.	Fixed prices	RATES	54.	Notion	IDEA
28.	Muse of lyric poetry	ERATO	55.	Household animals	PETS
29.	Clergyman's deputy	VICAR	58.	Contend	VIE
			59.	Epoch	ERA

Figure 33

can very easily become major problems if they aren't discovered in time and corrected immediately.

These two particular problems are a source of irritation, not only to the beginner but also to the experienced puzzle constructor as well—particularly if there is a tendency to get careless. However, you can avoid them if you take certain precautions when you fill in the diagram sections of the crossword puzzles.

The first problem—simple as it may seem—is usually caused by the use of misspelled words in the diagram section of the puzzle.

The solution to this problem is a simple one. Whenever you have any doubt about the correct spelling of a word, look it up in the dictionary. If you follow this practice faithfully, you will eliminate this problem completely—and will learn to spell many words correctly.

The second problem is usually caused by the use of identical words (or another form of the same word) in one diagram. Of course, this problem occurs more frequently in the larger size diagrams because of the larger number of words. It's more difficult to keep track of all the words in the large diagrams. On the other hand, if you get careless, this problem can occur quite frequently in the smaller diagrams too.

The solution to the second problem is also a simple one. You can very easily avoid the use of duplicate words (or other forms of the same words) in one diagram by double-checking each word in the diagram with the list of words on the proof sheet. You can compare each individual word twice—once before you enter the word in the diagram, and once after you transfer the same word from the diagram to the proof sheet.

The idea of comparing each individual word before you enter it in the diagram really isn't quite as difficult a task as it may appear at first. In fact, with the aid of a proof sheet, the first comparison—the most important one—can be completed in a matter of seconds.

The amazing thing about the proof-sheet method is that while it takes a long time to explain, it takes only a few seconds to accomplish.

I hope I will not be adding to your confusion, but in this section, instead of giving you specific instructions to follow, I am going to reverse the procedure and explain in full detail the manner in which I prepare and use the proof sheet in the construction of crossword puzzles. By reversing the procedure, I feel I can deviate slightly from certain specific steps which will allow me to make side comments on certain aspects of this method that I think are very important and should be explained in detail.

When you become familiar with the proof-sheet method for double-checking the words in the diagrams for duplicates, you may decide to adopt this method for your own use—that is, if you are completely satisfied with this method. On the other hand, if there are any particular steps you don't like, you can always change them to satisfy your own particular needs. Or perhaps the explanation of my proof-sheet double-checking method will give you a completely new idea on how to develop your own method for checking against duplicate words.

I've discovered, as you probably will if you get careless, that whenever I have tried to correct a misspelled word in the diagram, or whenever I have tried to change a duplicate word—that is, after the diagram was completely filled in—the correction has had a tendency to start a chain reaction which forced me to change a great number of words. And often, even after I had changed many words in the diagram, I still had the same problem. In fact, many times the problem had increased in size. However, I am happy to say that for me, this sort of problem is a thing of the past.

If you follow my proof-sheet method for double-checking the words in the diagram for duplicates—and, of course, there is no law or rule that says that you must—you will never be plagued by this particular problem.

Before I actually start to explain this proof-sheet method, I would like to point out that I'm going to explain it in a series of easy steps. For each step of the explanation, I'm going to use a reference number so that whenever I refer to a specific step (or steps), you will be able to find that step easily and quickly by the reference number(s).

Before I start to fill in any words in the rough diagram, I prepare a proof sheet in two easy steps:

1. I take a clean sheet of typewriter paper and divide it into nine equal sections, as shown in Figure 34.

2. I subdivide the nine sections on my proof sheet into smaller sections by printing certain letters of the alphabet in certain sections of the subdivisions.

The size of each subdivided section of my proof sheet depends, of course, on the size of the diagram and the number of words that begin with a specific letter of the alphabet. However, I have found in

A
ANILE—
AVE—
ARISE—
ATE●
ACE●

B
BORROWER●

C
CLEANEST●

D

E
EVER—
ETA—
ERATO●

F

G

H
HER●

I
INTO●
IRE●

L

M

N

O

P
PITCH—
PASS●

R
REVERE—
RATES●

S
SLAB—
STEER—
SODA
SOREHEAD—
STEVE●

T
TITO—
TACT
TIED●

V
VICAR●

W

Y

(41D and 41A)

Figure 34

the past that this particular layout (Figure 34) works quite well for all sizes of diagrams.

You will notice that on my proof sheet (Figure 34) I omitted the letters J, K, Q, U, X, and Z. The reason for this omission is the fact that I very seldom—if ever—use any words in my crossword puzzle diagrams that start with any one of these letters. On occasions when I must use words starting with any one of the missing letters, I manage to squeeze them in between the other words on my proof sheet.

You will also notice, on my proof sheet, that I allow less space beneath the letters F, G, H, and I. The reason for this is the fact that I also use very few words in my diagrams that start with any one of these four letters.

3. In the lower right-hand corner of the proof sheet, I print the serial number of my puzzle (this number will be fully explained in the next section) and the number of horizontal and vertical words in the crossword puzzle diagram (Figure 34).

(Before I go on to the next step, I would like to point out that I don't use my proof sheet until after I enter the first twenty-five or thirty words in the diagram section of my puzzle. The fact is that at this particular point I'm not too greatly concerned about using duplicate words—or other forms of the same word—in the same diagram because the first small number of words are grouped together in one particular corner of my diagram and I can very easily keep track of them. It's only after I enter the first group of twenty-five or thirty words in the diagram that I start to use my proof sheet.)

4. I fill in the first group of twenty-five or thirty words in my diagram, and then, I transfer them to my proof sheet.

5. First, I transfer all the words that are listed in the horizontal position of my diagram to my proof sheet. I draw a fairly large dot in the lower left-hand corner of the diagram square containing the first letter of the horizontal word that I wish to transfer to my proof sheet. In this particular case, the first square in my diagram contains the letter P in the first word PITCH (Figure 35). (This dot is a code symbol. Its principal function is to show that a specific word in the horizontal position of my diagram has been double-checked for duplicate words in the diagram, has been found to be acceptable, and has been transferred to my proof sheet.)

6. In this particular step, I transfer the first horizontal word (PITCH) from my diagram to my proof sheet—that is, I print the actual word (PITCH) on my proof sheet in the column directly be-

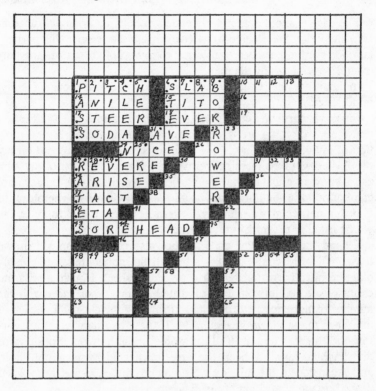

Figure 35

neath the letter P (Figure 34).

When there are many more words on my proof sheet, just before I actually print the transferred word from my diagram to my proof sheet, I glance at the specific column of words directly beneath that specific letter to see whether or not I have used the word previously.

Actually, when I transfer the word from my diagram to my proof sheet, this small additional step is the method I use to double-check each transferred word for duplicates. I use this same method to double-check both the horizontal and the vertical words in my diagram. This takes only a few seconds to perform, and since it has become a habit with me, I do it automatically. This habit is an easy one to acquire and I recommend it wholeheartedly.

7. After the word PITCH (on my proof sheet), I draw a dash, as shown in Figure 34.

The dash is another one of my code symbols. Its principal function is to show that the specific word (or words) that carries this particular code symbol has been transferred to my proof sheet from the horizontal position of my diagram.

In addition, this code symbol has two other functions of equal importance.

First, this particular code symbol (the dash) serves as an indication that the word on my proof sheet can be found in the horizontal position of my diagram. That is, if I wish to check a specific word on my proof sheet with the identical word in the diagram section of my puzzle, I know at a glance that the particular word carrying this symbol can be found in the horizontal position of my diagram. Therefore, to find this particular word in my diagram, I need to look only at the words listed in the horizontal position.

Second, this particular code symbol also serves as an aid in the horizontal word count. That is, after all the horizontal words in my diagram have been transferred to my proof sheet, I make a separate count of all the horizontal words listed on my proof sheet with the number of horizontal words listed in the lower right-hand corner of my diagram, as shown in Figure 34. If these two numbers don't correspond, then I know that all the words in the horizontal position of my diagram have not been properly transferred to my proof sheet, and I can locate the missing words merely by checking those listed in the horizontal position of my diagram.

In the same manner as explained in steps 5, 6, and 7, I transfer (to my proof sheet) all the remaining horizontal words in my diagram which aren't marked by a period in the lower left-hand corner of the square containing the first letter.

In the next three steps (8, 9, and 10), I will explain the method I use to transfer all the words from the vertical position of my diagram to my proof sheet.

8. I draw a fairly large dot in the upper right-hand corner of the square in my diagram that contains the first letter of the vertical word I wish to transfer to my proof sheet. (In this particular case, it's the first square in my diagram and contains the letter P in the word PASS, as shown in Figure 35.)

(The main reason for this dot in the upper right-hand corner of the square is that I also use it as a code symbol. This particular dot is placed in exactly the opposite corner of the square that also contains the dot representing the horizontal word PITCH. Its principal function is to show that this particular word, in the vertical position of my diagram, has been checked, has been found to be acceptable, and has been transferred to my proof sheet.)

9. In this step, I transfer the vertical word PASS from my diagram to my proof sheet—in the column directly beneath the letter P, as shown in Figure 34. (At this point, I also go through the additional step I had explained in the commentary of step 6.)

10. Directly after the word PASS (on my proof sheet), I draw a fairly large-size dot, as shown in Figure 34.

(This particular dot, which follows each vertical word on my proof sheet, is another one of my code symbols. Its principal function is to show that the word carrying the symbol has been transferred to my proof sheet from the vertical position of my diagram.)

This particular code symbol also has two other functions.

First, it indicates that that particular word can be found in the vertical position of my diagram. That is, if I wish to check a specific word on my proof sheet with the identical word in my diagram, I know at a glance that the particular word on my proof sheet carrying this symbol can be found in the vertical position of my diagram. Therefore, to find this identical word in my diagram, I need to look only at the words printed in the vertical position of my diagram.

Second, this code symbol also serves as an aid in the vertical word count. That is, after all the vertical words have been transferred from my diagram to my proof sheet, I make a count of all the vertical words listed on my proof sheet. The number of vertical words (41-D) on my proof sheet must correspond with the number of vertical words (41-D) listed in the lower right-hand corner of my diagram. If the two numbers don't correspond, then I know that all the words printed in the vertical position of my diagram have not been properly checked and transferred to my proof sheet, so I can find the missing words merely by checking those listed in the vertical position of my diagram.

In exactly the same manner as I have explained in steps 8, 9, and 10, I transfer (to my proof sheet) all the remaining words listed in the vertical position of my diagram—that is, all the vertical words that are listed in my diagram and are not marked with periods in the upper right-hand corners of the small squares containing the first letters of the vertical words.

11. If I wish to change a word in my diagram after it has been transferred to my proof sheet, I simply erase the word from both my

diagram and my proof sheet, and I print a new word in my diagram and immediately transfer it to my proof sheet.

12. After my first group of horizontal and vertical words (total of twenty-six) have been transferred from the diagram to the proof sheet, I fill in the next group of twenty-five or thirty words in the diagram; and then, I transfer them to my proof sheet in exactly the same manner as explained in steps 5, 6, 7 and in steps 8, 9, and 10.

13. After the first group of words (twenty-six words in this case) have been transferred from my diagram to my proof sheet, I perform one additional step just before I print each new word in my diagram. Each new additional word that I add to my diagram (after the first group of twenty-eight words) is double-checked for duplicate words in the diagram—once before I enter a new word in my diagram, and the second time when I transfer the new word from my diagram to my proof sheet. This additional step is performed in the following manner:

Let's assume, for example, that I wish to use the word STOVE in the diagram section of my puzzle. So just before I enter the word STOVE in my diagram, I glance at the column of words listed on my proof sheet beneath the letter S to see whether I had used this particular word previously in my diagram. This step takes only a few seconds to perform. If the word STOVE isn't already listed on my proof sheet in the S column, then I can safely use it in my diagram.

On the other hand, if the STOVE does appear on my proof sheet in the S column of words, then I know that I can't use this particular word in my diagram, because I will have two identical words in the same diagram. Therefore, I discard the word STOVE, select a new word, and go through the same procedure.

And, of course, just before I transfer the word from my diagram to my proof sheet, I go through the same procedure as explained in the commentary of step 6.

And just to prove to you that step 13 is a simple one to perform, I'm going to condense my explanation for step 13 into one short paragraph for clarity.

I select a word, and just before I print it in my diagram, I glance at a specific column of words on my proof sheet. If an identical word appears on my proof sheet, I discard the word and select a new one. But if the selected word doesn't appear in a specific column of words on my proof sheet, then I enter the word in my diagram and select the next word for my diagram.

Now perhaps you can see how each new word that is entered in my diagram is double-checked quickly and efficiently for duplicates in a matter of seconds.

When I am filling in a diagram, I find it most practical to work with small groups of twenty-five or thirty words at a time. After each new group of words that I transfer from my diagram to my proof sheet, I select a new group of twenty-five or thirty for my diagram. I follow this same procedure, over and over, until my diagram is completely filled in.

14. After my diagram has been completely filled in, and after all the words have been transferred from my diagram to my proof sheet, I count and compare the number of horizontal words and the number of vertical words listed in the columns of my proof sheet with the number of horizontal words (41-A) and the number of vertical words (41-D) listed in the lower right-hand corner of my proof sheet. If they correspond with one another, then I know that all the words in my diagram have been properly transferred to my proof sheet and that no duplicate words are in my diagram.

Ordinarily, step 14 completes the entire process for this particular operation. However, as an added precaution (and I might add that this extra step isn't necessary), I recheck all the words listed on my proof sheet for duplicates. So you see, I actually triple check each word in my diagram.

And now if this section still has you somewhat confused, perhaps I can simplify the whole procedure by listing the steps more concisely.

1. Prepare proof sheet (steps 1, 2, and 3).
2. Fill in the first group of twenty-five or thirty words in the diagram (step 4).
3. Transfer the first group of horizontal words from the diagram to the proof sheet (steps 5, 6, and 7).
4. Transfer the first group of vertical words from the diagram to the proof sheet (steps 8, 9, and 10).
5. Fill in the second group of twenty-five or thirty words in the diagram (step 12). (Before you actually start to fill in the second group of words in the diagram, read and follow step 13.)
6. Transfer the second group of horizontal words from the diagram to the proof sheet (steps 5, 6, and 7).
7. Transfer the second group of vertical words from the diagram to the proof sheet (steps 8, 9, and 10).
8. Continue this same procedure until the entire diagram is com-

pletely filled in with words.

9. If you wish to change a word in the diagram after it has been transferred to the proof sheet, read and follow step 11.

10. When the diagram is completely filled in and all the words have been properly double-checked and transferred to the proof sheet, count the number of horizontal words and the number of vertical words listed in the columns of the proof sheet.

11. Compare the number of horizontal words and the number of vertical words listed in the columns of the proof sheet with the number of horizontal and vertical words listed in the lower right-hand corner of the proof sheet and be sure that the numbers correspond with one another.

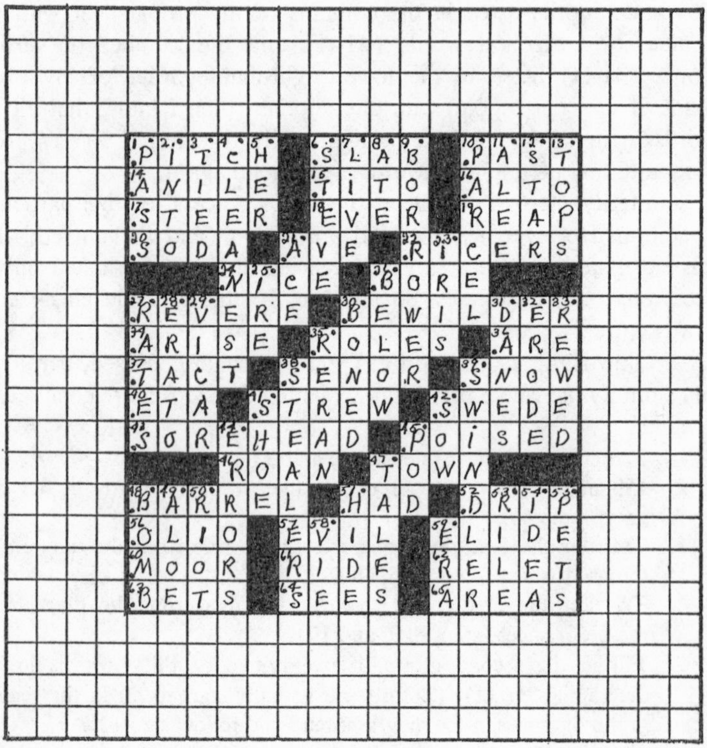

Figure 36

If you have any kind of difficulty in understanding this method, I suggest that you draw a small diagram, and fill it in with words using my proof-sheet method for double-checking for duplicate words in the diagram. After you go through the entire procedure of this method only once, you will have a thorough and complete understanding of the entire method—an understanding that you will not easily forget. You really have to try this method to be convinced. So try it, and be convinced.

HOW TO CONSTRUCT THE ROUGH CROSSWORD PUZZLE

At this point of the instructions, I feel that you should be thoroughly familiar with and able to mesh the basic components of a crossword puzzle. If you have carefully followed all the preceding instructions and comments in this book, you should feel confident enough to construct your first complete crossword puzzle.

Once again, in this particular section, and all the following sections, I'm going to reverse the instructions procedure. Instead of merely assigning specific instructions for you to follow, I'm going to explain to you in full detail, and step by step, the method I have developed to construct my own crossword puzzles. Here again, I feel that you will understand my method of constructing crossword puzzles much better, much quicker, and much easier if you follow along with me as I construct a complete puzzle.

First of all, I would like to point out that all types of puzzles are constructed in two stages—the rough stage and the finished stage.

Primarily, the rough stage of the puzzle is the preliminary stage, which must be completed before the finished puzzle—the one which is submitted to an editor—can be constructed. I simply call this preliminary puzzle a "rough" for want of a better name.

The truth of the matter is that when I prepare a rough diagram, I'm not the least bit fussy about the small details. For example, I roughly mark off and ink in all the black squares (unused squares) without any fuss or bother. If the black squares aren't completely inked in or if the ink flows over slightly into an adjoining white square, I don't worry too much about it.

I print the numbers roughly in the diagram with a pen and ink so that if I must do any erasing—and I usually do—the numbers in the diagram will not be erased. However, for easy erasing, I print the words in the rough diagram with a pencil.

My rough definition pages—numbers, definitions, and answer words—are also printed with a pencil for easy erasing.

I would like to point out the fact that when I construct the rough definition pages, I print the definitions rather than write them out in longhand. My reason for this is simple. I find that there is less chance for errors in spelling when I print. However, you may write the roughs out in longhand if you wish—if your handwriting is legible. Otherwise, I suggest that you print.

The illustrations in this book for the rough pages do not in the least resemble my roughs. They have been produced entirely in ink for reproduction purposes. Furthermore, an extra amount of care has been taken to keep these particular illustrations clean and legible. But regardless of how careless I get with the rough stages of my puzzles, I do take extra precautions to keep the finished puzzles clean, neat, and legible. For example, in the finished crossword puzzle, I'm exceptionally careful about all the small details. The diagram is carefully drawn and all the black squares are inked in solid. The numbers and the words are carefully typed in the diagram. Additional care is taken to keep the finished diagram page and the finished definition page free of ink smudges, dirty fingerprints, and noticeable erasures. These blemishes can greatly reduce the degree of quality and appeal of any type of word puzzle.

The rough diagrams I use for all sizes of crossword puzzles are 23×23. They were printed on a mimeograph machine and they are altered to suit my personal needs. I drew a sample copy of a 23×23 diagram which I took to a printer and had him run off five hundred copies.

The main reason I use the 23×23 diagrams for all of my rough puzzles is that these diagrams will take care of all puzzle sizes from a small 9×9 size to a large 23×23. In addition to the crossword puzzles, these same diagrams can be used as rough diagrams for the following types of puzzles: diagramless crossword puzzles, fill-in crossword puzzles, skeleton crossword puzzles, progressive blocks puzzles and the overlap crossword puzzles. For example, if I need a 15×15 size rough diagram, I simply mark off a 15×15 section of the 23×23 diagram. The smaller sections can be marked off from any one of the four corners of the 23×23 size; however, I prefer to mark off a suitable section directly from the center of the large diagram, as shown in Figure 36.

By using the 23×23 diagrams for all of my rough puzzles, I save a considerable amount of valuable time and money because I don't have to keep a variety of different-sized diagrams on hand. One diagram size takes care of all of my needs.

I find that the mimeographed diagrams are excellent to work on when they are used as roughs, but I don't recommend them for finished diagrams. For my finished diagrams, I always use diagrams drawn with pen and ink on smooth white bond paper. A well-drawn diagram—one that is drawn with good dark black ink lines—together with a good black typewriter ribbon that produces clear black numbers and words make an excellent combination to produce a professional-looking puzzle of a high quality.

I always submit at least five puzzles at one time—unless, of course, I fill out a specific order that may call for fewer. Therefore, I generally work on five puzzles at one time. I don't mean to imply that I work on them simultaneously. I work on them one after the other. For example, I prepare five rough diagrams—ink in the black squares, print the numbers with black ink, and fill in the diagrams with words. After the five rough diagrams have been completely filled in and found to be satisfactory, I print the rough definitions in the rough diagrams.

Whenever I work on a batch of puzzles at one time, I find that my mind is more alert, my chain of thought remains unbroken, and it is much easier for me to think of suitable words for my diagrams. (I work on the finished crossword puzzles in practically the same manner—five puzzles at one time.) However, if you are a beginner, I suggest that you work on one puzzle at a time until you really feel more confident.

For the particular demonstration in this section, I'm going to use a single 15×15 puzzle as an example. I feel that you will understand my method more clearly if you can focus your attention on a single crossword puzzle as I explain in full detail each step that I follow.

If, for example, I intend to submit a crossword puzzle—or any other type of word puzzle—to a particular publication for the first time, the first thing that I do is to purchase several different copies of the publisher's crossword puzzle magazines. (Practically all publishers in this business put out several different puzzle magazines each month.)

And the second thing that I do is to send for the publisher's requirement sheet.

In the meantime, however, while I'm waiting for the requirement sheet to arrive, I study the types of puzzles that are used in each magazine.

I have found, through personal experience, that it isn't enough for me just to study the different types of puzzles that appear in the crossword puzzle magazines. To become thoroughly familiar with the material in these magazines, I find that I receive the best results when I actually work on the puzzles. By solving several puzzles in each magazine, I become thoroughly familiar with the types of puzzles the publication uses, the types of words used in the diagrams, and the types of definitions used—plus the indication of form and usage.

When the requirement sheet for the crossword puzzle arrives, I study it until I become thoroughly familiar with the publisher's rules and requirements for constructing and submitting puzzles. Then, and only then, am I ready to begin constructing crossword puzzles for this particular publication.

The first thing I do when I begin to construct crossword puzzles is to select suitable diagram designs. As I have pointed out previously, and for obvious reasons, I always select my diagram designs from the magazines to which I intend to submit my puzzles. (In fact, I have been *instructed* by one editor to select my diagram designs from the crossword puzzle magazines which she edits.)

I don't select diagram designs for my puzzles at random. The fact is that I'm rather choosy about the selection of my diagram designs.

First, I select diagram designs that contain the minimum number of two- and three-letter words and the minimum number of long words. (Too many long words in the diagrams make them too difficult to fill in.)

Second, I select diagram designs that have only four- or five-letter words that cross each other in the corners.

Third, I avoid diagram designs in which the diagonal black squares run at an angle from left to right, as shown in Figure 29.

And fourth, I avoid all diagram designs starting with three-letter words. Most beginners aren't aware of the fact that practically all three-letter words are considered to be hackneyed words—trite words that are used excessively in many poor crossword puzzles. (When I first started to construct crossword puzzles, I used many different diagram designs that started with three-letter words because I found them so easy to fill in. However, I don't use them any more.)

One day, many years ago, a whole batch of my crossword puzzles were rejected and returned to me by a wonderful woman editor who helped me quite a bit to get started in this business. This particular editor was kind enough to enclose a short note along with the rejection slip. She informed me that I could improve the quality of my puzzles and make them more interesting simply by using less hackneyed words in my diagrams. And above all, she advised me not to start my crossword puzzles with hackneyed words. So I accepted her excellent advice graciously, and have followed it ever since.

Simply by observing this one rule, I must admit that I acquired an excellent batting average. It may be just a coincidence; nevertheless, I'm quite pleased with the over-all results.

Of course, a large number of crossword puzzles can be found that start with three-letter words—particularly in the smaller size puzzles. So evidently many editors do not object to this practice. If you feel that you want to use diagram designs starting with three-letter words, go right ahead. After all, my personal opinion could be wrong. However, after constructing hundreds of puzzles and having them published in a variety of crossword puzzle magazines, I get the feeling that I must be doing something right.

To prepare my rough diagram, I take one of my 23×23 mimeographed diagrams and mark off a 15×15 square section.

Mark an X with a pencil in every unused square (black square) in the rough diagram. And then, with a small artists brush (⚞3 red sable) and black waterproof India ink, roughly ink in all the squares that are marked with an X. (As I have previously explained, I spend very little time on this particular step of the puzzle.)

When all the black squares have been completely inked in and dried, take a fountain pen and print in all the required numbers in the proper white squares of the diagram.

Next, count the number of horizontal words in the diagram and make a notation of this number directly above and to the right of the rough diagram. And then count the number of vertical words in the diagram and make a notation of this number directly beneath the first number.

There are two reasons for this word count:

First, if an editor insists on having the word count listed on the diagram page, I will know at a glance (without recounting the words) the total number of words in the whole diagram.

Second, if I want to compare the number of definitions with the number of words in the diagram, I don't have to recount the number of words in the diagram—I just count the number of definitions in my puzzle, and if the number of definitions corresponds with the number of words in the diagram, I know that I have a definition for each word listed in the diagram.

In the lower right-hand corner of the rough diagram page I print my code number of the puzzle—say, 621. Besides confusing the editor, this code number is of no value to anyone but me and is listed on the diagram page for my personal use. For example, if I must refer to a specific puzzle for any reason, I can always locate the rough diagram page in my diagram file quickly merely by checking the code number. If one of my puzzles is rejected, or if I must rework a rejected puzzle before I can submit it to another publisher, I certainly have no difficulty locating the rough diagram page in my diagram file in order to make whatever changes are necessary.

If you decide to use a code number for your puzzles, by all means don't start with a low number—start with a fairly high number. Most editors are aware of the fact that many crossword puzzle constructors number their puzzles for identification purposes. And perhaps many editors are correct when they assume that the code number is actually the number of puzzles that a specific constructor has completed or submitted.

The whole idea behind the little game of code numbers is to try to leave the editor with the impression that you are an experienced professional in this field who has completed a large number of crossword puzzles. I must warn you, however, that the editors don't fool easily. So unless your puzzles are of a high quality, perhaps it would be best to forget about the code numbers until you really acquire some practical experience. However, if you do use a code number for your puzzles, don't make them too conspicuous. Use a pencil and print your code number lightly in small figures.

Before I actually start to fill in my rough diagram with words, I make up a proof sheet in exactly the same manner as explained in the preceding section.

Always start in the upper left-hand corner of the diagram, and then work to the right and down. As I enter each new word in the diagram, I check out the word for a duplicate. I double-check the same word for a duplicate when I transfer it from the diagram to my proof sheet in exactly the same manner as explained in the preceding section.

If there are any long words at the beginning of my diagram, I usually fill them in first.

After my rough diagram is completely filled in, I go over all the words in the diagram to see whether they are spelled correctly. Or sometimes I may decide to change a few of the existing words in my diagram—particularly if the words will make my puzzle more interesting and/or easier to solve.

When I'm satisfied with all the words in my rough diagram, I count the number of horizontal and vertical words listed on my proof sheet. I make a notation of these numbers in the lower right-hand corner of my proof sheet. If the number of words listed on my proof sheet corresponds with the number of words printed in my rough diagram, then I know that all the words that appear in my rough diagram have been transferred properly to my proof sheet.

When the two numbers have been verified and have been found to be correct, I print the words "checked OK" in the upper left-hand corner of my rough diagram page. Then I lay the rough diagram page aside for the time being and start to work on the rough definitions.

To prepare my rough definition pages, I draw three vertical lines on each definition page. These three lines separate the definition numbers and the definitions from the answer words. In the upper left-hand side of the first definition page I print the word ACROSS.

I copy the ACROSS definition numbers from the definition page of the puzzle I have selected for my diagram design. Or if I have designed my own diagram—which I do occasionally—I copy them directly from the diagram. These numbers are printed first on the definition page. Each number is followed by a period.

Next, I count the total number of definitions listed on the ACROSS definition page(s). I make a notation of this number directly beneath the last definition. Then I compare the number of definitions listed on the ACROSS definition page(s) with the number of horizontal words listed on my rough diagram page. If both numbers correspond with one another, then I know that I have a definition for every horizontal word listed in my rough diagram.

The DOWN definition page(s) for the rough definitions is prepared in exactly the same manner as the ACROSS definition page(s).

When both rough definition pages have been numbered correctly, I proceed to print my rough definitions (together with the answer words).

When both rough definition pages have been completed, I draw a bold line beneath definition ⧣25 on each rough definition page. If the ACROSS and the DOWN definitions have more than 50 or 75 definitions, I draw a bold line after the 25th, 50th, and 75th definitions. (When I start to type the finished definitions, these bold lines after each 25th definition will serve as a signal for me to start a new column of definitions—I type only 25 definitions to each column on the finished definition pages.

When all the rough definitions have been completed, I recheck for misspelled words. If all the definitions check out satisfactorily, I put the rough definition pages aside for the time being, and proceed to work on the finished stages of the crossword puzzle.

HOW TO CONSTRUCT THE FINISHED CROSSWORD PUZZLE

The first thing that I do when I construct a finished crossword puzzle is to draw a diagram with a pen and black permanent ink. (The page on which this diagram is drawn is called the diagram page.)

To complete the diagram design, I mark off and ink in (with black waterproof India ink) all the black squares (unused squares) in the diagram.

Whenever I do any work on the finished diagram page(s), I use a sheet of cardboard beneath the hand that rests on the finished diagram page. This sheet of cardboard prevents the diagram page from becoming smudged with dirty fingerprints. It also helps to prevent the diagram page from becoming warped from the heat and moisture of my hand.

When the ink is thoroughly dry in all the black squares, I insert the diagram page into the typewriter. In the upper right-hand corner of the diagram page (four spaces down from the top), I type my name, address, and the source of reference—the name of the dictionary I use. If a word count is required, I include this information directly beneath the source of reference.

Next, I type in all the required numbers in the proper squares of the diagram.

When all the required numbers have been typed in the diagram, I roll the diagram page back to the number 1 position in the first square of the diagram. And then I move one space to the right and one space to the bottom and proceed to type in all the words (in capitals) in the diagram.

When all the words are typed in the diagram, I take the diagram page out of the typewriter and print, with a pencil, my code number in the lower right-hand corner of the page. This particular step completes the finished diagram page. I lay this aside for the time being and start to type the definitions on the definition pages.

I find that the finished definition pages are quite simple to complete. It's merely a matter of copying the definitions correctly from the rough definition pages. (About the only difficulty I encounter in this particular step is an occasional typo.)

When I'm ready to type the definitions on the definition pages, I insert a clean sheet of paper into the typewriter. In the upper right-hand corner of each definition page, unless I'm instructed to do otherwise, I type my name and address (four spaces down from the top). (Incidentally, my name and address start in precisely the same spot on all of my diagram and definition pages. In fact, all the automatic stops on my typewriter are set in a fixed position so that my name, address, definition numbers, definitions, and the answer words are typed uniformly on all the definition and diagram pages.)

Eleven spaces down from the top of the definition page and ¾″ in from the left-hand side of the page, I type my first definition.

Two spaces above the first definition and in the center of the first column of definitions, I type the word ACROSS in capital letters. And then, I drop down two spaces below the first definition and proceed to type out the remaining ACROSS definitions. After the 25th definition (in the first column), I start my second column of definitions.

The DOWN definitions are typed in exactly the same manner as the ACROSS definitions.

In the lower right-hand corner of each definition page, I print (with a pencil) the code number of my puzzle. This step completes the finished crossword puzzle.

However, before I put my typewriter away, I usually go over the entire puzzle for one final check. I mostly look for misspelled words or wrong definition numbers. I also recount the number of definitions on each definition page just to make sure that I haven't skipped any.

The finished crossword puzzle is always submitted to an editor with the diagram page on top, the ACROSS definition page(s) next, and the DOWN definition page(s) on the bottom.

Never clip or staple crossword puzzles—or any type of word puzzles—together.

On the rough diagram page, directly above the diagram, I print the name of the publication to which my puzzles are submitted. In addition to the publisher's name, I also print the date that the puzzle is submitted. I keep this rough diagram in my file until my puzzle has been paid for, at which time, I discard it.

If any of my puzzles are rejected by a certain publication, I generally submit them to a different publication. However, before I submit the rejected puzzles to a different publication, I take the rough diagram pages out of my file. I cross out the old date of submission, together with the name of the publication that rejected my puzzles, and then I print a new submission date and the name of the new publication to which I intend to submit my rejected puzzles. After all the required information has been printed on my rough diagram page, I return the rough diagram pages to my file until further notice.

Incidentally, my file consists of three two-ring composition binders. Whenever I want to file any type of material, I simply punch two holes in the paper and file it in my two-ring binder. Besides filing my rough diagram pages, these binders are ideal for filing requirement sheets for crossword puzzles or any other kind of important correspondence. These binders are neat, compact, and take up very little space in my cabinet. And best of all, when I look for any kind of specific material in my file, I don't have to search through a stack of loose material. I simply pull out my two ring binders and all my filed material is laid out at my finger tips.

After the finished stage of the crossword puzzle has been completed and the rough diagram has been filed, the rough definition pages are discarded.

III How to Construct the Topical Crossword Puzzle

Topical crossword puzzles—sometimes called special-category crossword puzzles—are constructed in exactly the same manner as the regular crossword puzzle. The only noticeable difference between the topical and the regular crossword puzzle is that the topical one contains a certain number of words and definitions pertinent to one special category.

There is a demand by some publishers for crossword puzzles that are devoted to special subjects.

Topical crossword puzzles can be constructed in various sizes. However, the larger size diagrams are more suitable because they permit the constructor to use more of the special-category words. They are somewhat more difficult to construct than the ordinary puzzles, but the fact that most editors are willing to pay a higher rate for them—plus the fact that they stand a very much better chance of being accepted for publication—certainly makes the effort worthwhile.

There are thousands of special-category subjects to choose from—flowers, birds, wild life, marine life, seashore, TV stars, movie stars, trees, shrubs, insects, prominent people in the news, etc.

Stay away from special holiday themes, because these themes can be used in only one month out of the whole year. Furthermore, topical puzzles constructed around special holiday themes must be submitted to the publishers at least six months before the holidays actually arrive. I suggest that the special subject matter be appropriate for any day of the year.

If you find it somewhat difficult to find suitable special-category material (a list of words pertaining to a special subject matter), I suggest that you look over the special lists of words given for the fill-in puzzles found in most crossword puzzle magazines. These fill-in puzzles are based on special-category subject matter. The lists of special-category words used in these puzzles can also be used for topical crossword puzzles, and vice versa. In the fill-in puzzles, you will find many made-to-order lists of words pertaining to special categories. And, of course, you can add many of your own words to these lists in order to make them more adaptable to your own needs. Besides, adding your own words to these lists will give you a greater variety of words to choose from.

When you attempt to construct a topical crossword puzzle, the most important point to remember is that the entire puzzle—words and definitions alike—must be constructed around one special topic.

Let's assume, for example, that you want to construct a topical crossword puzzle around wild animals. The first thing which you must do before you start to construct the puzzle is to compile a long list of wild animal names (the longer the list the better).

List all the names of the animals in alphabetical order as well as by length. For example, list the three-letter names first, the four-letter names next, etc., as shown on the list in Figure 37.

Also bear in mind the fact that each one of the animal names can be changed to a plural form; thereby, giving you a double number of names to choose from. It also gives you a greater leeway in placing these names in the diagram section of the topical crossword puzzle. For example, you can put a three-letter name in a four-letter space merely by adding an "s."

The basic idea of the topical crossword puzzle is to use as many subject-matter words as possible. The definitions—as well as the names in the diagram section—must also be associated with the main topic. If the subject matter is wild animals, the following might apply:

1. Young bear   CUB
2. Wild male sheep   RAM
3. Antlered animal   DEER
4. American buffalo   BISON
5. Striped jungle cat TIGER
6. Timber wolf   LOBO

WILD ANIMALS

3	Lobo	Hyrax	Coyote	Gazelle	Wild boar
Ape	Lynx	Koala	Ermine	Gorilla	9
Cub	Mink	Lemur	Ferret	Lemming	Armadillo
Doe	Oryx	Moose	Gibbon	Leopard	Chickaree
Elk	Paca	Nagor	Gopher	Miniver	Orangutan
Fox	Pica	Okapi	Jackal	Muskrat	Springbok
Gnu	Slot	Otter	Jaguar	Opossum	Steinbock
Kid	Stag	Panda	Marmot	Panther	Thylacine
Ram	Titi	Ratel	Monkey	Polecat	Waterbuck
4	Topi	Sable	Muskox	Raccoon	10
Axis	Unau	Serow	Ocelot	Roebuck	Cacomistle
Bear	Wole	Shrew	Onager	Wallaby	Chimpanzee
Boar	Wolf	Skink	Rabbit	Wildcat	Rhinoceros
Buck	Zebu	Skunk	Vicuna	8	Wildebeast
Cavy	5	Stoat	Wapiti	Antelope	12
Cony	Addax	Tapir	Weasel	Capybara	Hippopotamus
Deer	Bison	Tiger	7	Elephant	
Fawn	Civet	Zebra	Aurochs	Kinkajou	
Guib	Coati	6	Blesbok	Chipmunk	
Hare	Daman	Agouti	Buffalo	Kangaroo	
Hart	Dingo	Baboon	Caraboa	Mandrill	
Ibex	Eland	Badger	Caribou	Mongoose	
Kudu	Genet	Beaver	Chamois	Pangolin	
Lion	Hyena	Cougar	Cheetah	Squirrel	

Figure 37

You will notice that each one of the preceding definitions is pertinent to the specific subject—wild animals.

Also keep in mind the fact that in the topical crossword puzzle there are many other words which though unrelated to a specific category (wild animals in this particular case) can also be used in the diagram section because they are somewhat associated with the main topic.

For example, words such as horn, antler, snare, trap, den, lair, forest, grass, trail, slot, spoor, paw, mane, hoof, etc., though not the names of wild animals are, nevertheless, related to the main topic. You can make many unrelated words in the diagram as important as the names of the wild animals, as shown in the following examples:

1.	Deer antler	HORN
2.	Elk horn	ANTLER
3.	Wild-animal trap	SNARE
4.	Wild-animal snare	TRAP
5.	Bear's lair	DEN
6.	Lion's den	LAIR
7.	Home of the deer	FOREST
8.	Buffalo food	GRASS
9.	Wild-game track	TRAIL
10.	Deer track	SLOT
11.	Wild-animal track	SPOOR
12.	Lion's foot	PAW
13.	Lion's neck hair	MANE
14.	Deer foot	HOOF

Even though the answer words in the preceding examples aren't names of wild animals, notice how their definitions are associated with the main topic of the puzzle—wild animals.

When you attempt to construct topical crossword puzzles, I would like to point out that not every word in the diagram section needs be related to the main topic. It's practically impossible to fill in a complete diagram with words that are related to a special category. So don't try for the impossible. The important thing to remember is to use as many words as possible of one category in the diagram section. Also try to slant as many definitions as you possibly can to your main topic. If, for example, you can use twenty-five or thirty words and definitions of a special category in one 23×23 puzzle, you can consider yourself quite lucky. However, the more words and definitions of a special category that you can use in a single topical crossword puzzle, the better your puzzle will be.

To really obtain the best results with the topical crossword puzzles, I suggest that you select diagrams that are designed to suit your specific needs—that is, select diagrams that are designed to match the lengths of the words you have compiled on a special category (wild animals in this particular case). For example, if most of the words on your list are three-, four-, and five-letter words, then select a diagram that is designed to accept the maximum number of three-, four-, and five-letter words. Or if most of the words on your list are four-, five-, and six-letter words, then select a diagram that is designed to accept the maximum number of four-, five-, and six-letter words, etc. The length of the words will vary from category to category, so just remember to select diagrams that are designed to suit the lengths of the words on your special-category list.

Whenever you use the name of a wild animal in the diagram section of the topical crossword puzzle, be sure to cross the name out on your list of wild animals so that you will not use it again in the diagram section of the puzzle. However, if you happen to slip up somewhere along the line, your proof sheet will prevent you from using duplicate names in the diagram.

The finished diagram page for the topical puzzle is prepared in exactly the same manner as for the regular puzzle, with one exception. In order to point out (to the editor) that the crossword puzzle you are submitting is constructed around a special category, type the words (in capitals) TOPICAL CROSSWORD PUZZLE about eight or ten spaces above the diagram on the finished diagram page. Two spaces below the title of the puzzle, type the title of your special category, as shown in the following example:

TOPICAL CROSSWORD PUZZLE
(Wild Animals)

And that is about all there is to the topical crossword puzzle.

Every time that you compile a new list of words pertaining to a special category, I suggest that you type the list of words on a clean sheet of paper and put it away in your file for future use in other puzzles. Never throw any list of words away. Remember that you can use the same list of words over and over for other puzzles. Besides being adaptable to topical puzzles, this same list of words can also be used to construct fill-in puzzles, which are quite popular with many puzzle fans.

The fill-in puzzle, which will be explained in another chapter, is also constructed around a special category.

IV How to Construct the Diagramless Crossword Puzzle

The diagramless crossword puzzle is simply a regular crossword puzzle in which the numbers and the boxes have been omitted from the diagram. This type of puzzle is easy to construct, but very difficult to solve because the puzzle solver is called upon to plot the diagram in addition to finding the correct synonyms for the given definitions.

Even though there are many diagramless crossword puzzles published in puzzle magazines, I can assure you that very few are ever completely solved by puzzle solvers. However, this fact has no bearing whatsoever on the crossword puzzle constructor. The fact remains that the editors do purchase them and pay a fairly good rate for them. So as long as the editors are willing to accept them, I suggest that you construct them and submit them with other types of word puzzles.

Diagramless crossword puzzles are constructed and submitted to the editors in exactly the same manner as regular crossword puzzles. In fact, the only noticeable difference between the diagramless and the regular crossword puzzle is the fact that the diagramless variety usually contain only about one half to two thirds the number of words in their diagrams. And since there are fewer words used in the diagramless crossword puzzles, there also are fewer definitions to contend with. As a rule, you will find that approximately one half (or slightly less) of the squares in the diagrams of the diagramless crossword puzzles are blacked out.

Because the diagramless puzzles are easier to construct than the regular crossword puzzles, you will find that the editors usually pay lower rates for them. However, even though the rates are somewhat lower, it pays to construct them whenever they are in demand because it takes only about half the time to complete them.

The diagramless puzzles can be constructed in various sizes. They are usually constructed in smaller sizes, such as 13×13 and 15×15. Nonetheless, it's not unusual to find diagramless crossword puzzles of the larger sizes, such as 17×17, 19×19, and 21×21.

There are some editors who take regular crossword puzzles and convert them into diagramless puzzles simply by printing blank diagrams in which the numbers and the black squares are omitted. Why the editors do this is a mystery to me. Perhaps it's because they

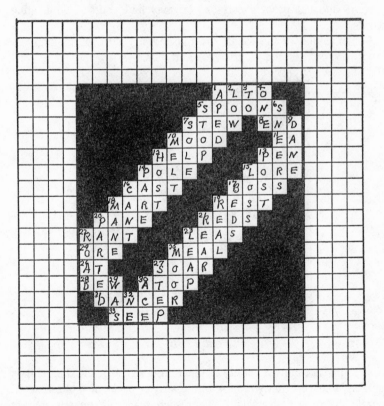

Figure 38A

don't receive enough diagramless puzzles to meet their demands. On the other hand, I've seen diagramless crossword puzzles that had been converted into regular puzzles. So you see, one can never be sure just what certain editors will do with different types of word puzzles.

Before you actually start to construct diagramless crossword puzzles, let me remind you, once again, that they are constructed in exactly the same manner as the regular puzzles—that is, they are constructed in both the rough and the finished stages.

For the smaller sizes, the proof sheet may be omitted. Because of the small number of words in the smaller diagrams, there really isn't any difficulty in keeping track of all the words to prevent duplication. (For the larger sizes of these types of puzzles, I suggest that you prepare and use proof sheets or you may find yourself duplicating words.)

For examples of the rough and finished stages of the diagramless crossword puzzles, see Figures 38A and 38B.

Figure 38B

If you wish to find a variety of diagram designs for the diagramless puzzles, I suggest that you look in the answer pages of the crossword puzzle magazines. Practically every such magazine on the market publishes several diagramless crossword puzzles each month. For additional diagram samples, see Figures 40 and 41.

John Doe, Jr.
1635 Woodland Rd.
Cannon, Va. 11776

ACROSS			DOWN	
		1.	Mimicked	APED
1. Lowest female voice	ALTO	2.	Opposite of high	LOW
		3.	Toward	TO
5. Pieces of tableware	SPOONS	4.	Single thing	ONE
		5.	Cease	STOP
7. Boil slowly	STEW	6.	Scoffs	SNEERS
8. Terminate	END	7.	Shoe bottom	SOLE
10. Disposition	MOOD	9.	Native of Denmark	DANE
11. Each (abbr.)	EA	10.	Thaw	MELT
12. Aid	HELP	12.	Landlord	HOST
13. Coop	PEN	13.	Mail	POST
14. Fishing rod	POLE	14.	Remove the rind	PARE
15. Learning	LORE	15.	Waste	LOSS
16. Throw	CAST	16.	Dialect	CANT
17. Foreman	BOSS	17.	Sleeping places	BEDS
18. Emporium	MART	18.	Lion's neck hair	MANE
19. Relax	REST			
20. Window glass	PANE	19.	Genuine	REAL
21. Communists	REDS	20.	Separated	PARTED
22. Rave	RANT	21.	Hindmost	REAR
23. Meadows	LEAS	22.	Highway	ROAD
24. Metallic rock	ORE	23.	Jump	LEAP
		25.	Anchor	MOOR
25. Dinner or lunch	MEAL	27.	Pace	STEP
26. Nearby	AT	29.	Existed	WAS
27. Glide in air	SOAR	30.	High card	ACE
28. Morning moisture	DEW	32.	Compass point (abbr.)	NE
30. On the top	ATOP			
31. Ballerina	DANCER			
33. Ooze	SEEP			

Figure 39

Figure 40

Figure 41

When you complete the finished stages of the diagramless crossword puzzles, discard the rough definition pages but keep the rough
diagram pages for your record.

V How to Construct the Make-It-Yourself Crossword Puzzle

The make-it-yourself crossword puzzle—sometimes called the fill-in puzzle—is a simple variation of the regular crossword puzzle. In this type of puzzle, there are no numbers printed in the diagram section of the puzzle and no definitions are given for the answer words. Instead, the puzzle solver is given a lead word in the diagram and a list of words arranged in alphabetical order according to the number of letters in each word. To solve this type of puzzle, the puzzle solver must try to fit the list of given words into their proper squares in the numberless diagram.

The make-it-yourself crossword puzzle is another one of those puzzles that are difficult to solve. Therefore, it hasn't quite reached the degree of popularity that the regular crossword puzzle has attained.

Because the numbers and the definitions are omitted in the make-it-yourself crossword puzzles, you will find that this type of puzzle is somewhat easier to construct than the regular one.

As a rule, no abbreviations are permitted in the make-it-yourself crossword puzzles.

This particular type of puzzle can be constructed in a variety of sizes. However, like the diagramless puzzle, the make-it-yourself puzzle is usually constructed in the smaller sizes—usually in the 13×13 or 15×15 sizes.

Because of its small size this kind of puzzle usually consists of two pages—the diagram page and the word page, as shown in Figures 42 and 43.

```
S T A R ■ M O L A R ■ P O L E
P I L E ■ A D O R E ■ A R I A
E R M A ■ R E N E W ■ R A N T
D E A L E R S ■ N E S T L E S
■ ■ T R Y ■ L A D E N ■ ■ ■ ■
D O N O R ■ R E S ■ P E A R S
O V E R ■ I A N ■ B A R R E L
V I A ■ A D M I R A L ■ S E A
E N R A G E ■ E A R ■ L O F T
R E S I N ■ A N N ■ H A N S E
■ ■ L E A S T ■ H A N ■ ■ ■ ■
A R R E S T S ■ M A S T E R S
B O O R ■ L E V E R ■ E D I T
L O B O ■ A R I S E ■ R I T E
E D E N ■ S T E A M ■ N E A P
```

Figure 42

The make-it-yourself crossword puzzle, like any other type of word puzzle, is also constructed in two stages—the rough stage and the finished stage.

The finished diagram page consists of a diagram with all the black squares inked in solid. The white squares in the diagram, as in the regular crossword puzzle, must be keyed to one another. All the words must be typed in capitals in the diagram. Your name, address, and the source of reference—the name of the dictionary that you use —must be given in the upper right-hand corner of the diagram page. And, of course, if you use a code number, it is printed (with pencil) in the lower right-hand corner of the diagram page.

The finished word page must also include your name and address in the upper right-hand corner (unless you are instructed by an editor to do otherwise). The words (usually in capitals) must be listed in alphabetical order according to the number of letters in each word. All the words must be double-spaced with the columns of words reading up and down (Figure 43) rather than across.

And, here again, for the make-it-yourself crossword puzzle—and for all the following types of puzzles covered in this book—I'm going to reverse the procedure of instructions. That is, instead of giving you specific instructions to follow, I'm going to explain in full detail the simple method I have developed and use to construct this kind of puzzle.

John Doe, Jr.
1635 Woodland Rd.
Cannon, Va. 11776

3-Letters	Edie	Agnes	6-Letters
Ann	Edit	Arise	Arenas
Bar	Erma	Arson	Assert
Ear	Line	Atlas	Barrel
Err	Lobo	Donor	Enrage
Han	Loft	Dover	7-Letters
Has	Mesa	Hanse	Admiral
Ian	Neap	Harem	Aileron
Ide	Odes	Laden	Arrests
Lon	Oral	Least	Dealers
Ram	Over	Lever	Lantern
Ran	Pile	Marry	Lenient
Res	Pole	Molar	Masters
Sea	Rant	Nears	Nestles
Try	Rita	Ovine	Partner
Via	Rite	Pears	Realtor
Vie	Robe	Reefs	
4-Letters	Rood	Renew	[82]
Able	Sped	Resin	
Alma	Star	Rewed	
Aria	Step	Sepal	
Boor	Tire	Slate	
Eats	5-Letters	Steam	
Eden	Adore		

Figure 43

By all means, don't be afraid to experiment with other kinds of construction methods. I don't guarantee that my method is the best method known or the perfect method. I merely say that it is the best method I have discovered. Use whatever method is most suitable for your own needs, just as long as the results are the same.

The method I use is explained in the following fifteen easy steps:

1. I select a suitable 15×15 diagram design which contains the minimum number of spaces which are designed to accept three-letter words.

(Occasionally, you may find make-it-yourself puzzles that contain two-letter words in the diagram sections. Personally, I avoid them.)

2. To prepare my rough diagram, I take one of my mimeographed 23×23 size diagrams and mark off a 15×15 section.

3. I roughly ink in all the black squares in the rough diagram; however I omit the numbers in this particular diagram because they are unnecessary in the make-it-yourself crossword puzzle.

4. Above the diagram, on the rough diagram page, I print the number of horizontal words and the number of vertical words in the diagram. In the lower right-hand corner of this page, I print the code number of my puzzle (630).

5. I prepare a proof sheet for my puzzle.

6. Constantly checking my proof sheet for duplicate words, I fill in the rough diagram in exactly the same manner as I fill in the regular crossword puzzle—in small groups of words with about twenty-five or thirty words to each group of words.

(As a rule, abbreviations aren't permitted in the make-it-yourself puzzles. There are times when this rule may be broken, but I recommend that you avoid them in your make-it-yourself puzzles.)

7. As in the regular crossword puzzle, when my rough diagram for the make-it-yourself puzzle is completely filled in with suitable words, I make a word count of all the horizontal words and all the vertical words listed on my proof sheet to make sure that the number of words listed on my proof sheet jibes with the list on the rough diagram page. If both numbers correspond with one another, I make a notation of this fact ("checked OK") in the upper left-hand corner of the rough diagram page. This step completes the rough diagram page.

8. To prepare my rough word page, I compile separate lists of all the three-, four-, five-, six-, seven-, and eight-letter words that are listed on my proof sheet. It is a good idea to list the number of letters in each word on your proof sheet. Noting the particular number after each word makes it simple to separate the various word lengths at a glance.

9. Next, I take a clean sheet of paper and print, in alphabetical order, separate lists of three-, four-, five-, six-, seven-, and eight-letter words. (See Figure 44.)

10. I count the number of words listed on the rough word page to be absolutely sure that I haven't skipped any. Then, I make a notation of the total number of words (82) directly beneath the last word on the rough word page. This particular step completes the rough stage of the make-it-yourself crossword puzzle.

11. The finished diagram page for this type of puzzle is constructed in exactly the same manner as the diagram page for the regular crossword puzzle, with one exception—the numbers are omitted in the diagram section.

12. About eight or ten spaces above the diagram, and in the center of the diagram page, I print (in capitals) the name of the puzzle. This step completes the diagram page.

13. To produce a finished word page, I insert a clean sheet of

John Doe, Jr.
1635 Woodland Rd.
Cannon, Va. 11776

3-Letters	EDIE	AGNES	6-Letters
ANN	EDIT	ARISE	ARENAS
BAR	ERMA	ARSON	ASSERT
EAR	LINE	ATLAS	BARREL
ERR	LOBO	DONOR	ENRAGE
HAN	LOFT	DOVER	
HAS	MESA	HANSE	7-Letters
IAN	NEAP	HAREM	ADMIRAL
IDE	ODES	LADEN	AILERON
LON	ORAL	LEAST	ARRESTS
RAM	OVER	LEVER	DEALERS
RAN	PILE	MARRY	LANTERN
RES	POLE	MOLAR	LENIENT
SEA	RANT	NEARS	MASTERS
TRY	RITA	OVINE	NESTLES
VIA	RITE	PEARS	PARTNER
VIE	ROBE	REEFS	REALTOR
	ROOD	RENEW	
4-Letters	SPED	RESIN	
ABLE	STAR	REWED	
ALMA	STEP	SEPAL	
ARIA	TIRE	SLATE	
BOOR		STEAM	
EATS	5-Letters		
EDEN	ADORE		

Figure 44

paper into the typewriter. In the upper right-hand corner I type my name and address.

14. Eleven spaces down from the top of the word page (¾″ in from the left-hand side), I type the words double-spaced in columns. (Wider margins could have been used on the word page; however, as I have pointed out previously, all of my automatic stops on my typewriter are set in a fixed position. Therefore, I have used the ¾″ margin on the left-hand side of the word page.)

John Doe, Jr.
1635 Woodland Rd.
Cannon, Va. 11776

ACROSS	STAR	NESTLES	SPED	LENIENT
3-Letters			STEP	PARTNER
ANN	5-Letters	DOWN	TIRE	REALTOR
EAR	ADORE	3-Letters		
HAN	ARISE	BAR	5-Letters	
IAN	DONOR	ERR	AGNES	
RES	HANSE	HAS	ARSON	
SEA	LADEN	IDE	ATLAS	
TRY	LEAST	LON	DOVER	
VIA	LEVER	RAM	HAREM	
	MOLAR	RAN	MARRY	
4-Letters	PEARS	VIE	NEARS	
ARIA	RENEW		OVINE	
BOOR	RESIN	4-Letters	REEFS	
EDEN	STEAM	ABLE	REWED	
EDIT		ALMA	SEPAL	
ERMA	6-Letters	EATS	SLATE	
LOBO	BARREL	EDIE		
LOFT	ENRAGE	LINE	6-Letters	
NEAP		MESA	ARENAS	
OVER	7-Letters	ODES	ASSERT	
PILE	ADMIRAL	ORAL		
POLE	ARRESTS	RITA	7-Letters	
RANT	DEALERS	ROBE	AILERON	
RITE	MASTERS	ROOD	LANTERN	

Figure 45

15. When all the words have been typed on the word page, I count the total number of words (82) in order to be absolutely sure that I haven't skipped any. This particular step completes the make-it-yourself crossword puzzle.

Before I lay the completed puzzle aside, I usually like to go over it again for one final check. In the final check, I look for misspelled words.

There are some editors who prefer to have the ACROSS and the DOWN lists of words typed separately on the word page, as shown in Figure 45.

Whenever I must keep the ACROSS and the DOWN lists separated on the word pages, I prepare my rough word pages in the manner as shown in Figure 45. By preparing them in this manner, I find that there is less tendency to make any errors when I type the finished word pages.

If a publisher doesn't have a requirement sheet for the make-it-yourself crossword puzzles but still uses them in his crossword puzzle magazines, I suggest that you construct your make-it-yourself puzzles in exactly the same manner as they appear in the publisher's magazines. Then you can't go wrong.

VI How to Construct the Chain Word Puzzle

The chain word puzzle—sometimes called the overlap word puzzle or the clapboard word puzzle—is really nothing more than a regular crossword puzzle in which the black squares are omitted in the diagram.

The chain word puzzle is another one of those puzzles that are very difficult to solve, but this one, I hastily add, is also very difficult to construct. Perhaps for these reasons very few are published in to-day's crossword puzzle magazines. In addition, the prevailing rates for these types of puzzles are entirely too low for the amount of time that it takes to construct them.

The chain word puzzle is constructed in exactly the same manner as the regular crossword puzzle.

There are two outstanding features about the chain word puzzles: (1) the black squares are omitted in the diagrams, and (2) the last letters of the preceding words are actually the first letters of the following words.

Notice, for example, in Figure 46 that the last letter of the first word (SERENADED) is actually the first letter of the following word (DINAR).

You may find it somewhat difficult to keep track of the words in the rough diagram—that is, knowing where one word ends and where the next word begins. However, if you use the proof-sheet method for checking the words in the diagram for duplicates, you will not have too much difficulty because the dots (code symbols) in the corners of the squares that contain the first letters of the horizontal and the vertical words in the diagram will definitely show, without any doubt, where the horizontal and the vertical words begin and end.

The most important point that you must remember about this particular type of puzzle is that the last letter of each preceding word must be the first letter of each following word. If you keep this fact in mind, you will not have too much difficulty in constructing the chain word puzzle.

In this type of puzzle, the rough diagram is made up of ½" squares. The reason for the larger squares in this particular diagram is the fact that I like to print the words in the diagram somewhat larger in size for the chain word puzzle than for the regular crossword puzzle diagram. As you know, the diagram for the chain word puzzle has no black squares to separate the individual words in the diagram. So, I like to print the words large enough in the rough diagram so that I can distinguish the individual words clearly.

S	E	R	E	N	A	D	E	D	I	N	A	R
T	R	A	D	E	D	E	B	U	T	I	L	E
A	R	I	E	L	A	L	O	N	E	L	I	A
R	O	S	A	L	I	E	N	O	M	E	N	D
T	R	E	T	O	M	O	O	R	I	V	E	R
S	E	A	R	O	O	S	T	A	L	E	R	A
T	A	R	O	N	O	E	R	I	O	T	O	G
O	R	A	T	E	S	E	E	D	R	O	S	S
P	E	N	T	E	E	S	P	A	I	N	E	T
E	D	I	E	D	E	N	A	G	S	A	R	A
R	I	N	D	I	M	A	N	E	L	M	E	L
A	N	T	E	M	I	R	E	N	E	E	L	K
P	E	O	N	E	V	E	W	E	D	D	A	S

Figure 46

Figure 47

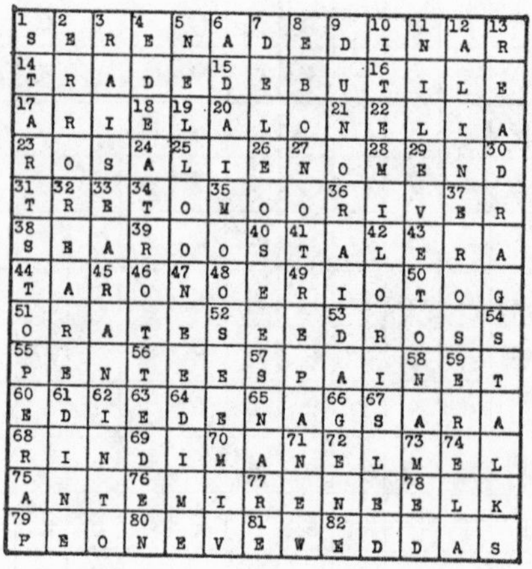

1 S	2 E	3 R	4 E	5 N	6 A	7 D	8 E	9 D	10 I	11 N	12 A	13 R
14 T	R	A	D	E	15 D	E	B	U	16 T	I	L	E
17 A	R	I	18 E	19 L	20 A	L	O	21 N	22 E	L	I	A
23 R	O	S	24 A	25 L	I	26 E	27 N	O	28 M	29 E	N	30 D
31 T	32 R	33 E	34 T	O	35 M	O	O	36 R	I	V	37 E	R
38 S	E	A	39 R	O	O	40 S	41 T	A	42 L	43 E	R	A
44 T	A	45 R	46 O	47 N	48 O	E	49 R	I	O	50 T	O	G
51 O	R	A	T	E	52 S	E	E	53 D	R	O	S	54 S
55 P	E	N	56 T	E	E	57 S	P	A	I	58 N	59 E	T
60 E	61 D	62 I	63 E	64 D	E	65 N	A	66 G	67 S	A	R	A
68 R	I	N	69 D	I	70 M	A	71 N	72 E	L	73 M	74 E	L
75 A	N	T	76 E	M	I	77 R	E	N	E	78 E	L	K
79 P	E	O	80 N	E	V	81 E	W	82 E	D	D	A	S

Figure 48

John Doe, Jr.
1635 Woodland Rd.
Cannon, Va. 11776

ACROSS

1.	Wooed with music	SERENADED	
9.	Iranian coin	DINAR	
14.	Bartered	TRADED	
15.	First appearance	DEBUT	
16.	Floor covering	TILE	
17.	Arabian gazelle	ARIEL	
19.	Musical syllable	LA	
20.	By oneself	ALONE	
22.	Charles Lamb	ELIA	
23.	Girl's name	ROSA	
24.	Foreigner	ALIEN	
27.	City in Alaska	NOME	
29.	Terminate	END	
31.	Waste allowance	TRET	
34.	Short for Thomas	TOM	
35.	Anchor a ship	MOOR	
36.	Large stream	RIVER	
38.	Scorch	SEAR	
39.	Perch	ROOST	
41.	Fairy story	TALE	
43.	Epoch	ERA	
44.	Edible rootstock	TARO	
46.	Forward	ON	
47.	Negative reply	NO	
48.	Over (poet.)	OER	
49.	Tumult	RIOT	

50.	Coat (sl.)	TOG
51.	Harangues	ORATES
52.	Sow	SEED
53.	Refuse of metal	DROSS
55.	Confined	PENT
56.	Golf mounds	TEES
57.	European country	SPAIN
58.	Mesh fabric	NET
60.	Short for Edith	EDIE
63.	Biblical garden	EDEN
65.	Old horses	NAGS
67.	Girl's name	SARA
68.	Orange peel	RIND
69.	Obscure	DIM
70.	Lion's neck hair	MANE
72.	Shade tree	ELM
73.	Honey (pharm.)	MEL
75.	Poker stake	ANTE
76.	Arabian ruler	EMIR
77.	Girl's name	RENEE
78.	Wapiti	ELK
79.	Sp. Amer. laborer	PEON
80.	Granular snow	NEVE
81.	Female sheep	EWE
82.	Norse literary works	EDDAS

Figure 49

John Doe, Jr.
1635 Woodland Rd.
Cannon, Va. 11776

DOWN

1.	Begins	STARTS	34. Jogged	TROTTED
2.	Mistake	ERROR	35. Lowings of	
3.	Elevate	RAISE	a cow	MOOS
4.	City in		36. Foray	RAID
	Nigeria	EDE	37. Saw-	
5.	Girl's		toothed	EROSE
	name	Nell	38. Cease	STOP
6.	Girl's		40. Observes	SEES
	name	ADA	41. Surgical	
7.	Delete	DELE	saw	TREPAN
8.	Like		42. Girl's	
	ebony	EBON	name	LORIS
9.	Press for		43. Short	
	payment	DUN	jacket	ETON
10.	News		45. Hindu	
	article	ITEM	queen	RANI
11.	River in		47. Require	NEED
	Egypt	NILE	52. Appear to	
12.	Bring into		be	SEEM
	line		53. ---- Ham-	
	(var.)	ALINE	mar-	
13.	Peruse	READ	skjold	DAG
18.	Consume		54. Stems	STALKS
	food	EAT	55. For each	PER
20.	Point a		57. Trap	SNARE
	gun	AIM	58. Nominated	NAMED
21.	Likewise		59. Before	ERE
	not	NOR	61. Have	
25.	Diving		dinner	DINE
	bird	LOON	62. To the	
26.	Gr. God-		inside	INTO
	dess of		64. Small coin	DIME
	dawn	EOS	66. Short for	
27.	Negative		Eugene	GENE
	word	NOT	67. Snow	
28.	Wire		vehicle	SLED
	measure	MIL	68. Knock on	
29.	Adam's		door	RAP
	mate	EVE	69. Cozy room	DEN
30.	Pulls		70. Roman 1004	MIV
	along		71. Novel	NEW
	behind	DRAGS	74. Guido's	
32.	Raised	REARED	highest	
33.	Hearing		note	ELA
	organ	EAR		

Figure 50

When filling in the rough diagram of a chain word puzzle, I try to work with as few words as possible at one time. Generally, there are many words that are erased or changed around in the diagram section of this type of puzzle before the diagram is actually filled in completely. Therefore, I don't print any numbers in the diagram until the diagram is completely filled in and checked out properly.

As in the regular crossword puzzle, I print a dot (code symbol) in the lower left-hand corner of each square that contains the first letter of each horizontal word listed in the diagram. And I print a dot in the upper right-hand corner of each square that contains the first letter of each vertical word listed in the diagram.

These specific code symbols not only show me where the horizontal and the vertical words begin but also point out the proper squares in the diagram in which a number must be printed. For example, when the diagram section of the chain word puzzle is completely filled in with suitable words, I simply start at the first square in the diagram (working from left to right) and print the required number in each square that contains a dot (or two).

Figures 46 and 47 show the completed rough stages of the chain word puzzle. And Figures 48, 49, and 50 show the finished stage of the same puzzle.

If you can't get any requirement sheets for chain word puzzles from the publishers, I suggest that you study the chain word puzzles in their puzzle magazines and then construct your own in exactly the same manner (and style).

Before I close this chapter, I would like to give you a piece of advice—forget it! Stay away from these particular types of puzzles. Stick to the regular crossword puzzles and you will be further ahead in the long run. The only reason I include the chain word puzzle in this book is simply to give you a general idea of how this particular type of crossword puzzle is constructed. Perhaps someday you may wish to include one in a group of sample puzzles you are submitting to an editor whom you wish to impress with the different types of word puzzles you are capable of constructing.

VII   How to Construct the Progressive Blocks Puzzle

The progressive blocks puzzle is somewhat different from a regular crossword puzzle. In the progressive blocks puzzle the answer words in the diagram do not cross one another as they do in the regular crossword puzzle. Instead, they start in the first block of the diagram and travel clockwise around the diagram interlocking with the next block.

Progressive blocks puzzles are usually constructed in one of two sizes—15×15 or 19×19. I have never seen them constructed in the 23×23 sizes. Perhaps it's because they have never been offered in these sizes to the editors of crossword puzzle magazines.

Progressive blocks puzzles are quite easy to construct. In fact, I think these particular puzzles are much easier to construct than diagramless crossword puzzles of the same size because the diagram sections of the progressive blocks puzzles contain a smaller number of words. For example, a 15×15 size progressive blocks puzzle contains only 16 answer words and 16 definitions. The 19×19 size contains only 25 answer words and 25 definitions.

There really isn't too much work involved in the construction of progressive blocks puzzles. You simply follow the publisher's rules and instructions set forth in the requirement sheet for these puzzles. If the publisher doesn't have a requirement sheet for this type of puzzle (and many don't) but still uses them in his puzzle magazines, study the publisher's magazines to see what method he uses. Once you understand the make-up of any type of word puzzle, you will find that it really isn't too difficult to figure out the publisher's style and setup simply by studying identical puzzles in his puzzle magazines.

In the progressive blocks puzzle the seventh letter of each word in the diagram (with the exception of the first word, of course) is actually the first letter of the following word. For example, in Figure 51 you will notice that the last letter of the first word (CAREENED) is the letter "D," which also happens to be the first letter of the second word in the diagram (DIVERSIONS). And the seventh letter of the second word (DIVERSIONS) is the letter "I," which also happens to be the first letter of the third word (INSTIGATED), etc.

For the progressive blocks puzzles, as for many of the other types of word puzzles, different publishers use different styles and setups. For example, you will find that some crossword puzzle magazines give the puzzle solvers only the definitions for the answer words in the diagrams, as shown in the following examples:

DEFINITIONS
1. Lurched
2. Pastimes
3. Incited

And some crossword puzzle magazines, in addition to the definitions, also give the missing letters of the answer words. The missing letters of the answer words are typed in alphabetical order to the right of the definitions, as shown in the following examples:

DEFINITIONS	MISSING LETTERS
1. Lurched	A-E-E-E-N-R
2. Pastimes	I-E-N-O-R-S-S-V
3. Incited	D-E-G-I-N-S-T-T

However, when you submit progressive blocks puzzles, you must remember that they also need the answer words which must be listed on the definition pages, as shown in Figures 51 and 52.

I have pointed out that the progressive blocks puzzle isn't too difficult to construct. However, in order to give you a much better understanding of this particular type of puzzle, I will give you a general idea of the procedure that I follow when I construct a 15×15

John Doe, Jr.
1635 Woodland Rd.
Cannon, Va. 11776

DEFINITIONS   WORDS

  1. Lurched   CAREENED
  2. Pastimes   DIVERSIONS
  3. Incited   INSTIGATED
  4. Suite of rooms   APARTMENTS
  5. Talebearer   TATTLETALE
  6. Train schedules   TIMETABLES
  7. Reverse stroke   BACKSTROKE
  8. Kind of drum   KETTLEDRUM
  9. Acts of deserting   DESERTIONS
10. Pertaining to idealism   IDEALISTIC
11. Established the identity of   IDENTIFIED
12. One's native land   FATHERLAND
13. Embroidery   NEEDLEWORK
14. Fairylike imaginary realm   WONDERLAND
15. Device for cracking nuts   NUTCRACKER
16. Excluded   ELIMINATED

Figure 51

size progressive blocks puzzle.

1. I send for a requirement sheet for progressive blocks puzzles and when the requirement sheet arrives, I study it in order to become thoroughly familiar with the publisher's construction rules and requirements. In addition to the requirement sheet, I also study the progressive blocks puzzles in the publisher's puzzle magazines.

2. I prepare a 15×15 size rough diagram. (And, here again, you will notice that for my rough diagram, I use one of my large 23×23 mimeographed diagrams in which I mark off a 15×15 section.

3. I mark off and ink in all the black squares in the diagram.

4. With pen and ink, I print all the necessary numbers from 1 to 16 in the proper squares of the rough diagram.

5. I prepare a proof sheet. (Incidentally, even though this particular puzzle contains only 16 words in the diagram section, I still use a proof sheet. However, this particular proof sheet is somewhat

John Doe, Jr.
1635 Woodland Rd.
Cannon, Va. 11776

DEFINITIONS	WORDS	MISSING LETTERS
1. Lurched	CAREENED	A-E-E-E-N-R
2. Pastimes	DIVERSIONS	I-E-N-O-R-S-S-V
3. Incited	INSTIGATED	D-E-G-I-N-S-T-T
4. Suite of rooms	APARTMENTS	A-E-M-N-P-R-S-T
5. Talebearer	TATTLETALE	A-A-E-E-L-L-T-T
6. Train schedules	TIMETABLES	A-E-E-I-L-M-S-T
7. Reverse stroke	BACKSTROKE	A-C-E-K-O-R-S-T
8. Kind of drum	KETTLEDRUM	E-E-L-M-R-U-T-T
9. Acts of deserting	DESERTIONS	E-E-N-O-R-S-S-T
10. Pertaining to idealism	IDEALISTIC	A-C-D-E-I-L-S-T
11. Established the identity of	IDENTIFIED	D-D-E-E-I-I-N-T
12. One's native land	FATHERLAND	A-A-D-E-H-L-R-T
13. Embroidery	NEEDLEWORK	D-E-E-E-K-L-O-R
14. Fairylike imaginary realm	WONDERLAND	A-D-D-E-L-N-O-R
15. Device for cracking nuts	NUTCRACKER	A-C-C-K-R-R-U-T
16. Excluded	ELIMINATED	A-D-E-I-I-L-M-N-T

Figure 52

different from the one for the regular crossword puzzle. On the proof sheet for the progressive blocks puzzle, I simply list the answer words in a single column. Because of the small number of words in this type of puzzle, there is very little chance of using duplicate words in the diagram.)

6. I fill in the rough diagram with 16 suitable words, and in order to make the puzzle as easy as possible to solve, I select simple words that require simple definitions.

7. I prepare the rough definition page. If the requirement sheet for this type of puzzle calls for the missing letters of the answer words to be listed, or if the magazine shows that the missing letters of the an-

swer words listed, then I list them on my rough definition page in the following manner:

(a) I eliminate (from the list of missing letters) the two letters of each word that fall in the numbered squares. For example, I eliminate the letter "C" which falls into square number 1 and the letter "D" which falls into square number 2 as shown in the following example:

Example:
–AREENE–

(b) I arrange the remaining letters of each answer word in alphabetical order (A-E-E-E-N-R) and list them on the rough definition page to the right of the answer.

When the rough stage of my progressive blocks puzzle is completed, I count the number of definitions to be sure I haven't missed any. In addition, I go over all the words to be sure that they are all spelled correctly.

8. In order to complete the finished stage of the puzzle, I draw a 15×15 diagram and ink in all the black squares. (As I have pointed out previously, I always take extra care to keep my finished puzzle— diagram and definition page(s)—free of smudges, erasure marks, dirty fingerprints, etc.)

9. When the ink is thoroughly dry in the black squares of the diagram, I insert the page into the typewriter. In the upper right-hand corner, I type my name, address, and source of reference.

10. I drop down to the diagram and type in all the necessary numbers in the proper squares of the diagram (Figure 53).

11. I roll the diagram page back to the first square of the diagram and proceed to type in the words in capitals.

12. When the diagram page is completed, I take it out of the typewriter and print the code number of my puzzle in the lower right-hand corner (Figure 54). This step completes the diagram page.

13. I insert the definition page into the typewriter and type my name, address, definition numbers, definitions, and the answer words, as shown in Figure 51.

14. When the definition page is completed, I take it out of the typewriter and print the code number of my puzzle in the lower right-hand corner.

This last step completes the finished stage of the progressive blocks

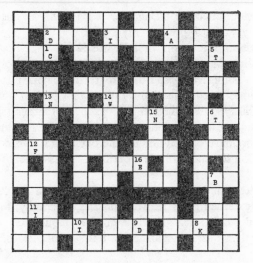

Figure 53

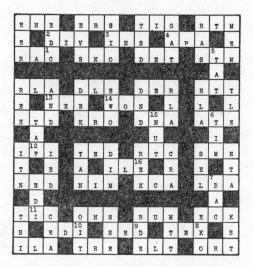

Figure 54

puzzle. However, before I lay it aside, I like to go over the entire puzzle—diagram and definition page—to be sure that all the definitions are listed and that all the words are spelled correctly.

If the missing letters of the answer words must be listed on the definition page, then I prepare my rough definition page and the finished definition page as shown in Figure 52.

Before I bring this chapter to a close, I would like to point out that just because a publisher doesn't use progressive blocks puzzles in any of his magazines doesn't necessarily mean that he will not purchase puzzles of this type. The reason for the lack of progressive blocks puzzles in many of the magazines may be due to the fact that no puzzle constructors have offered any for the publisher's consideration. So it does no harm to send out a few occasionally as feelers to different publishers.

On the other hand, some publishers adhere to a fixed rule; they purchase only certain types of word puzzles. Generally, they list the types of word puzzles they purchase on their requirement sheets, on the covers of their puzzle magazines, or on their mastheads.

VIII   How to Construct the Fill-in Puzzle

The fill-in puzzle (sometimes called the crosspatch, word-a-gram, crossbone, skeleton, or framework) is just another variation of the regular crossword puzzle. It's somewhat similar to the make-it-yourself crossword puzzle, because it doesn't include any definitions.

In order to solve the fill-in puzzle, a list of words is given to the puzzle solver who must select and transfer to the diagram a series of given words. When all the given words have been placed correctly in their proper squares in the diagram, the words will read from left to right and from top to bottom. In order to get the solver started, a lead word is given in the diagram section.

There seems to be a great demand for fill-in puzzles. Many puzzle fans seem to like these puzzles much better than the regular crossword puzzles; many publishers put out magazines that are devoted exclusively to fill-in puzzles.

Fill-in puzzles, like topical crossword puzzles, are constructed from a series of words that are pertinent to a specific subject. And, as in the regular crossword puzzles, all the words in the diagrams must lock with one another.

Generally, publishers of puzzle magazines have requirement sheets for fill-in puzzles. However, when you request requirement sheets for this type of puzzle be sure to ask for it by the name under which they are published in that particular magazine. For example, if a certain publisher lists this type of puzzle as a skeleton puzzle, then you must request a requirement sheet for the skeleton puzzle.

As I have pointed out, some publishers are quite generous with the amount of information they furnish concerning the rules and requirements for specific types of puzzles that they purchase. The opposite is also true. So if there is any important information lacking in the requirement sheets, you can always pick it up by studying the same types of puzzles in the publisher's magazines.

The diagrams for the fill-in puzzles, just like the regular crossword puzzles, are symmetrical in design—that is, they are square. They are constructed in a variety of sizes, such as 16×16, 17×17, 18×18, 19×19, 21×21, and sometimes in the 25×25 square sizes.

Generally, you will find that publishers use diagrams of a specific size for their fill-in puzzles. For example, one publisher may use only 19×19 size diagrams for all of his fill-in puzzles, while another publisher may use only 21×21 diagrams. Occasionally you may find a publisher who may use two different sizes of diagrams for his fill-in puzzles. However, this is an exception rather than a rule.

And, of course, you may even find a publisher who uses two different methods for presenting the word lists for fill-in puzzles. But, here again, this is an exception rather than a rule.

Usually, there are no single black squares permitted in the diagram sections of the fill-in puzzles. Two black squares is the minimum number that is permitted in a single group of black squares in the diagrams. You may find a publisher who breaks this rule by allowing the use of single black squares in the diagram section. However, I recommend that you use two black squares as the minimum number of black squares in a single group.

Fill-in puzzles, just like any other types of word puzzles, are constructed in two stages—the rough stage and the finished stage.

The finished diagram page consists of a diagram with all the black squares inked in solid. The words (in capitals) must be typed. Your name, address, and the source of reference must appear in the upper right-hand corner of the diagram page. The name of the puzzle (in capitals) and the title of the special category should be placed above the diagram—approximately eight or ten spaces. If a code number for the puzzle is used, it is placed in the lower corner of the diagram page.

The finished word page must include your name and address in the upper right-hand corner. The words (all of one category) must be double-spaced and listed alphabetically in groups of three-letter words, four-letter words, etc. The columns of words must read vertically rather horizontally.

Generally, you will find that the diagram pages of the fill-in puzzles, just as the diagram pages of the regular crossword puzzles, are constructed and printed the same in all the crossword puzzle magazines. However, the word pages of the fill-in puzzles, like the definition pages of the crossword puzzles, vary in construction from publisher to publisher.

For example, some requirement sheets for fill-in puzzles may instruct you to type the word lists in capital letters, as shown in the following examples:

3 LETTERS	4 LETTERS	5 LETTERS
APE	BEAR	BISON
CUB	BOAR	CIVET
DOE	DEER	DINGO
ELK	FAWN	ELAND
FOX	LION	GENET
GOA	LOBO	MOOSE

Some requirement sheets for fill-in puzzles may instruct you to capitalize only the first letter of each word, as shown in the following examples:

3 LETTERS	4 LETTERS	5 LETTERS
Ape	Bear	Bison
Cub	Boar	Civet
Doe	Deer	Dingo
Elk	Fawn	Eland
Fox	Lion	Genet
Goa	Lobo	Moose

Some requirement sheets may instruct you to list the numbers (3, 4, 5, etc.) and the word LETTERS in a manner as shown in the following examples:

#1:
3-Letters   4-Letters   5-Letters

#2:
3 Letters   4 Letters   5 Letters

⌗3:
3-Letter Words   4-Letter Words   5-Letter Words

⌗4:
3-LETTERS   4-LETTERS   5-LETTERS

And to be somewhat different, some requirement sheets may instruct you to type the word lists in the manner as shown in the following examples:

3-APE	4-DEER	3-ELK	3-GOA
4-BEAR	5-DINGO	4-FAWN	4-LION
5-BISON	3-DOE	3-FOX	4-LOBO
6-COUGAR	5-ELAND	5-GENET	5-MOOSE

(Notice that in the preceding examples the words are listed in alphabetical order regardless of the number of letters in the individual words.)

Fill-in puzzles are quite easy to construct; I don't think you will have any difficulty with them. I have developed my own simple method for constructing them. The method works quite well for me, and I'm sure that when you become accustomed to it, it will work as well for you.

1. I study the publisher's requirement sheet for fill-in puzzles, in order to become thoroughly familiar with his rules and requirements. I also study the publisher's magazines in order to become familiar with his format.

2. I select a suitable category and compile a large list of words (the more the better) pertinent to the subject. The words are arranged in alphabetical order according to the number of letters in each word, as shown in Figure 55.

(Incidentally, you will notice that the category I have selected to illustrate the fill-in puzzle is the same category—wild animals—I had used to explain the construction of the topical crossword puzzle. When my fill-in puzzle is completed, I file my list of wild animal names for future use in other fill-in and topical crossword puzzles.)

3. When I have a complete list of words selected, I prepare a 17×17 square rough diagram. Here again, you will notice that I have used one of my large 23×23 size mimeographed diagrams on which I have marked off a 17×17 square section. You will also notice that

WILD ANIMALS

3	Lobo	Hyrax	Coyote	Gazelle	—Wild boar
—Ape	Lynx	Koala	—Ermine	Gorilla	
Cub	Mink	Lemur	—Ferret	Lemming	9
Doe	Oryx	—Moose	Gibbon	Leopard	Armadillo
—Elk	Paca.	—Nagor	Gopher	Miniver	Chickaree
—Fox	Pica	Okapi	Jackal	Muskrat	—Orangutan
—Gnu	Slot	—Otter	—Jaguar	Opossum	Springbok
Kid	Stag	Panda	Marmot	Panther	Steinbock
Ram	—Titi	Ratel	Monkey	Polecat	Thylacine
	Topi	Sable	Muskox	—Raccoon	—Waterbuck
4	Unau	Serow	Ocelot	Roebuck	
Axis	Wole	Shrew	—Onager	Wallaby	10
Bear	Wolf	Skink	—Rabbit	—Wildcat	Cacomistle
Boar	Zebu	Skunk	Vicuna		Chimpanzee
Buck		Stoat	—Wapiti	8	Rhinoceros
—Cavy	5	Tapir	Weasel	—Antelope	—Wildebeest
—Cony	Addax	—Tiger		Capybara	
Deer	—Bison	Zebra	7	—Elephant	12
Fawn	Civet		Aurochs	Kinkajou	Hippopotamus
Guib	—Coati	6	Blesbok	Chipmunk	
Hare	Daman	—Agouti	Buffalo	—Kangaroo	
Hart	—Dingo	—Baboon	—Caraboa	Mandrill	
—Ibex	Eland	—Badger	Caribou	Mongoose	
Kudu	Genet	Beaver	Chamois	Pangolin	
Lion	Hyena	Cougar	Cheetah	Squirrel	—Wildebeast

Figure 55

my rough diagram (Figure 56) has no black squares inked in. The black squares aren't necessary in the rough diagram at this point. In fact, until the rough diagram is filled in with a suitable number of words, I never know where the black squares will fall into the diagram.

4. From my special category list of wild animal names, I fill in as many names as I possibly can into my rough diagram. I start with the longest names first, then work down to the shorter names, because the shorter names are more readily adaptable to the smaller areas of the diagram. I usually fill in the outside squares of the diagram first, and then, work down to the center of the diagram. Occasionally I change the names around in the diagram until the best position for a specific name is located.

5. Every time that I use a name in the diagram section of my puzzle, I draw a small dash in front of the identical name on my list of wild animal names, as shown in Figure 55. These small dashes in-

```
W  I  L  D  E  B  E  A  S  T  .  W  A  P  I  T  I
I  .  .  I  .  .  .  .  .  .  A  .  B  .  .  .
L  .  O  N  A  G  E  R  S  .  T  I  G  E  R  S
D  .  G  .  E  .  .  A  .  .  E  .  X  .  .  .
C  F  O  X  .  K  A  N  G  A  R  O  O  .  .  W
A  E  .  .  .  .  .  O  .  .  B  .  T  I  T  I
T  R  A  B  B  I  T  U  .  .  U  .  T  .  .  L
.  R  .  .  A  .  .  T  .  .  C  E  .  .  .  D
B  E  .  .  B  .  .  I  .  .  K  R  .  .  .  B
A  N  T  E  L  O  P  E  S  .  .  .  .  .  .  O
D  .  L  .  O  .  J  .  C  A  R  A  B  O  A  .
G  .  E  .  N  .  A  O  A  .  .  .  .  .  .  R
E  A  P  E  .  G  .  G  .  N  C  A  V  Y  .  .
R  .  H  .  .  N  .  U  .  Y  .  C  .  .  .  .
.  O  R  A  N  G  U  T  A  N  .  M  O  O  S  E
.  .  N  .  .  .  .  R  .  .  .  O  .  .  .  .
C  O  A  T  I  .  B  I  S  O  N  .  N  A  G  O  R
```

Figure 56

dicate that the names on the list that carry these dashes have already been used in the diagram; therefore, duplicating names in the same diagram is practically impossible. If for any reason I decide to remove a name from the diagram, I simply erase the name from the diagram and the dash that precedes the identical name on my list of wild animal names.

6. After my rough diagram has been filled in, I check the names in the diagram with the names on my list (the ones marked with a dash) to be sure that I haven't used any duplicated names in the diagram.

7. I count the number of names in my rough diagram and make a notation of this count above and to the right side of the diagram. In the upper left-hand corner of the diagram page, I print the words "checked OK." In the lower right-hand corner of the same page, I print the code number (640) of my puzzle.

8. On my rough word page, I print (in alphabetical order and arranged according to the number of letters in each name) a complete list of the names that are used in the diagram section of the puzzle. (This particular step is a simple one; I start at the top of the three-

letter column of names on my list and copy each name that is marked off by a dash. This method automatically arranges the names in alphabetical order and in groups of three-, four-, five-, six-, seven-, eight-, nine-, and ten-letter words.)

9. Directly beneath the last word listed on the rough word page, I print the total number of words on the page. In the lower right-hand corner of the same page, I print the code number of my puzzle. This step completes the rough word page. (Incidentally, before I lay the rough word page aside and start working on the finished stage of the puzzle, I make sure that the number of names listed on the rough word page corresponds with the number of names listed on the rough diagram page. If the number of names checks out correctly, I lay the rough puzzle aside and start to work on the finished stage.

10. I draw a 17×17 size diagram. However, at this point, I do not ink in any black squares in the diagram.

11. I insert the diagram page into the typewriter. In the upper right-hand corner I type my name, address, and the source of reference.

W	I	L	D	E	B	E	A	S	T		W	A	P	I	T	I
I			I								A			B		
L		O	N	A	G	E	R	S			T	I	G	E	R	S
D			G			L			A		E			X		
C		F	O	X		K	A	N	G	A	R	O	O			W
A		E							O		B		T	I	T	I
T		R	A	B	B	I	T		U		U		T			L
		R			A				T		C		E			D
B		E			B				I		K		R			B
A	N	T	E	L	O	P	E		S							O
D			L		O			J		C	A	R	A	B	O	A
G			E		N			A		O		A				R
E		A	P	E		G		G		N	C	A	V	Y		
R			H			N		U		Y		C				
	O	R	A	N	G	U	T	A	N		M	O	O	S	E	
			N					R				O				
C	O	A	T	I		B	I	S	O	N		N	A	G	O	R

Figure 57

12. Approximately eight or ten spaces above the diagram, I type the name of the puzzle and the title of the category.

13. I drop down to the first square in the diagram, place the first square in the proper position in the typewriter and proceed to type (in capitals) the names of the wild animals in the diagram (Figure 57).

(Incidentally, when I start to type the names in the diagram section of the puzzle, I really have no specific method to follow—that is, I may type one name in the diagram that may read from left to right, and the next name that I type in the diagram may read from top to bottom. After the first word is typed in the diagram, I go from one interlocking word to another regardless of what direction the word may read. I usually type in the direction that is most practical. Once I establish the proper position for the first name in the diagram, I can move the diagram page in any direction—up, down, left, or right—as many times as I wish without changing the position of any of the names in the diagram, and when I'm finished with the diagram, all of the names will line up perfectly.)

14. After all the names have been typed in the diagram, I remove the diagram page from the typewriter and ink in all the black squares, as shown in Figure 58.

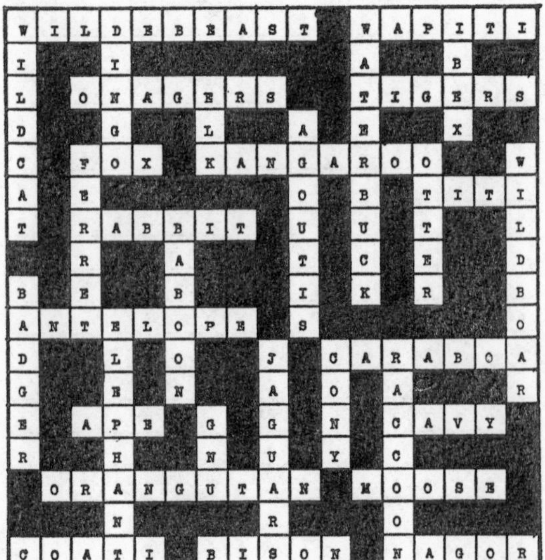

Figure 58

(Incidentally, the black squares may be inked in either before or after the names have been typed in the diagram. However, I prefer to ink them in after because there is less chance of inking in the wrong squares.)

15. I then count the total number of names in the diagram to be sure that I haven't skipped any. If the number of names in the diagram checks out correctly, I print (with a pencil) the code number of my puzzle in the lower right-hand corner of the diagram page and put it aside.

16. I insert a clean sheet of paper into the typewriter. (This sheet of paper is called the word page.) In the upper right-hand corner of the word page, I type my name and address (Figure 59).

```
                                    John Doe, Jr.
                                    1635 Woodland Rd.
                                    Cannon, Va. 11776
```

```
3-LETTERS    6-LETTERS
APE          BABOON      8-LETTERS
ELK          BADGER      ANTELOPE
FOX          FERRET      ELEPHANT
GNU          RABBIT      KANGAROO
             TIGERS      WILD BOAR
4-LETTERS    WAPITI
CAVY                     9-LETTERS
CONY         7-LETTERS   ORANGUTAN
IBEX         AGOUTIS     WATERBUCK
TITI         CARABOA
             JAGUARS     10-LETTERS
5-LETTERS    ONAGERS     WILDEBEAST
BISON        RACCOON
COATI        WILDCAT
DINGO
MOOSE
NAGOR
OTTER
```

Figure 59

17. One inch in from the left-hand side of the word page, eleven

spaces down from the top, I proceed to type the names of the wild
animals, as shown in Figure 59. (All the names are double-spaced,
they are arranged in alphabetical order and listed according to the
number of letters in each name. Of course, if the requirement sheet
calls for only the first letter of each name to be capitalized, then I
prepare my word page as shown in Figure 60.

John Doe, Jr.
1635 Woodland Rd.
Cannon, Va. 11776

3-LETTERS	6-LETTERS	8-LETTERS
Ape	Baboon	Antelope
Elk	Badger	Elephant
Fox	Ferret	Kangaroo
Gnu	Rabbit	Wild boar
	Tigers	
4-LETTERS	Wapiti	9-LETTERS
Cavy		Orangutan
Cony	7-LETTERS	Waterbuck
Ibex	Agoutis	
Titi	Caraboa	10-LETTERS
	Jaguars	Wildebeast
5-LETTERS	Onagers	
Bison	Raccoon	
Coati	Wildcat	
Dingo		
Moose		
Nagor		
Otter		

Figure 60

18. When the word page has been completed, I take it out of the
typewriter and count the total number of names listed on the page in
order to be sure that I haven't skipped any. If the total number of
names checks out correctly, I print the code number of my puzzle in
the lower right-hand corner of the page. This step completes the
finished stage of the fill-in puzzle. However, before I am completely
satisfied, I go over the entire puzzle once more in order to be sure

that all the words are spelled correctly.

When the finished puzzle checks out to my satisfaction, I discard the rough word page but retain the rough diagram page for my record.

Before I put my list of wild animal names in my file for future use, I erase all the dashes that appear before the names on the list.

The fill-in puzzle can also be constructed without any black squares showing in the diagram, as shown in Figure 61. This type of diagram design requires a little extra time to complete, as opposed to the diagram design shown in Figure 58. And I might add that even though the puzzle shown in Figure 61 is more professional looking

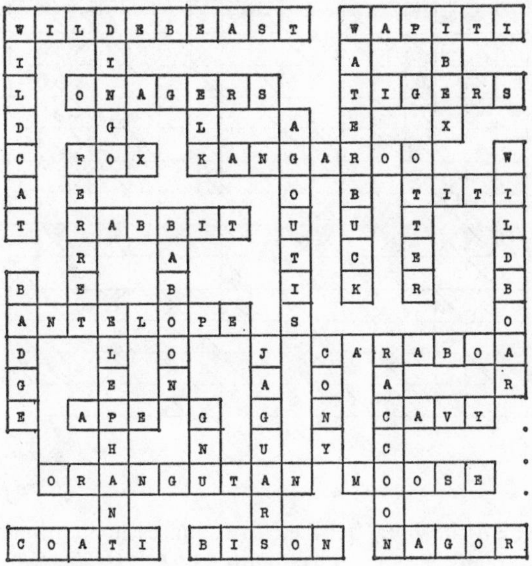

Figure 61

than the one shown in Figure 58, it will not add any extra money to your monthly check.

Although it isn't necessary, whenever I submit a sample fill-in puzzle to an editor for the first time, I always submit the sample puzzle with two diagram designs—one with the black squares inked in and one with the black squares omitted. With the sample puzzle, I enclose a short note to the editor in which I inform him that I can construct any number of fill-in puzzles with either one of the two diagram designs. I ask the editor which diagram design he prefers.

The diagram design, as shown in Figure 61, in which all the black squares have been eliminated, is drawn in five simple steps:

1. I outline a regular 17×17 size diagram with dots.

2. I take the diagram page out of the typewriter, and "X" in the diagram (very lightly) with a pencil, as shown in Figure 62.

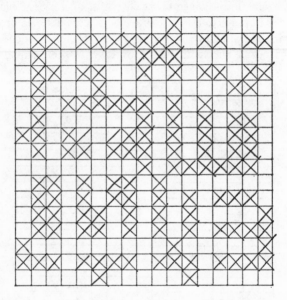

Figure 62

3. I erase all the lines between the squares in the diagram which must remain blank, as shown in Figure 63.

4. With the aid of a ruler, I trace all the lines in the diagram with a pen and ink.

5. When the inked lines are completely dry, I erase whatever pencil lines remain on the traced diagram, and the result is a diagram design without any black squares.

Try drawing a few sample diagram designs of this type. You will find that they aren't nearly as difficult to draw as they may appear at first.

This particular diagram design (Figure 63), as I have pointed out previously, will not bring in any higher rates for your fill-in puzzles;

however, it does give the puzzle a professional-looking appearance—which may help to sell more of your fill-in puzzles.

An excessive amount of black space in the diagram sections of fill-in puzzles gives the diagram pages a dark, drab appearance. Of course, this is only my opinion, and I could be wrong. However, if I were an editor who had a choice of selecting either one of the two diagram designs, I certainly would select the diagram design with no black squares. I would select the design shown in Figure 63.

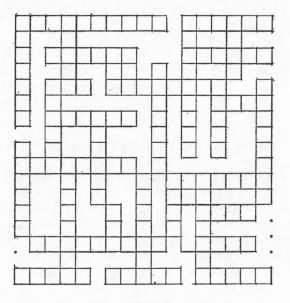

Figure 63

IX How to Construct the Acrostic Puzzle

Acrostic puzzles, like the fill-in puzzles, can be found in many different crossword puzzle magazines under a variety of different names, such as crostigrams, diocrostics, wordograms, web-crostics, quotewords, and perhaps a few other names which I may not be familiar with. Even though the names of these puzzles may differ from one publisher to another, the basic construction procedures and the rules for solving them are the same.

Of all the different word puzzles, the acrostic puzzles are the most difficult ones to solve, and, I might add, the most difficult of all word puzzles to construct.

In order to solve an acrostic puzzle, the puzzle solver must first find the correct answer word (synonym) for each given definition. Then, each numbered letter of the answer word must be transferred to an appropriate square in the diagram. If the puzzle is completed properly, the diagram, reading from left to right, will form a quotation from a published book or article. In addition, the first letters of the answer words will spell out the author's name and the work from which the quotation was taken.

The most difficult part about solving acrostic puzzles is the fact that the solver has no way of knowing whether the answer words for the given definitions are correct until all the letters of the answer words have been transferred to the diagram.

Before you actually attempt to construct and submit any acrostic puzzles, you must be thoroughly familiar with the publisher's rules and requirements. For example, some publishers use short quotations for acrostic puzzles and some use long quotations. Some publishers use quotations that are written in prose, while others use quotations written in verse. Some use quotations that are of a serious nature; others prefer humorous ones. Generally you will find that the long quotations are written in prose.

The acrostic puzzle is usually constructed and slanted exclusively to meet the requirements of a specific publication. Therefore, there is little you can do with a reject. There are really only two options: You can discard it and forget about it, or you can put it away in your file for a few months and then resubmit it to the same publication for another try.

Many of the publishers of crossword magazines will send you requirement sheets for acrostic puzzles on request. Bear in mind that this type of puzzle is also published under a variety of names by different publications. So when you request requirement sheets, be sure you ask for requirement sheets by the names under which they are published. If a certain publisher calls an acrostic a quoteword puzzle, then you must request a requirement sheet for a quoteword puzzle. And don't forget to include a stamped, self-addressed envelope with your request.

In addition to the information that is given in the requirement sheets, you will also have to study the acrostic puzzles in the publisher's puzzle magazines because the publishers don't give out too much information on this type of puzzle.

Though, as I have pointed out, acrostic puzzles are the most difficult of all word puzzles to construct, I hope that I didn't discourage you to the point of giving up. They are difficult, but the fact remains that acrostic puzzles are being constructed and sold every day of the year. So don't give them up without giving yourself a chance.

The ability to construct all types of word puzzles will help you to get established with the editors of crossword puzzle magazines. When the editors find that you can construct all types of interesting word puzzles of a high quality—beginners or otherwise—they will purchase your puzzles.

The diagrams used for acrostic puzzles are drawn somewhat differently from those used for regular crossword puzzles. For example, the regular crossword puzzle diagrams are symmetrical (square) in design, whereas, the diagrams for the acrostics are oblong.

If you study the acrostic puzzles published in different puzzle magazines, you will find that the over-all sizes vary from one publication to another. For example, some publications use small diagrams, such as 15×8 squares, and some publications use large ones, such as 21×14 squares. (The first number of a given size shows the width of the diagram; the second number shows the depth of the diagram. That is, a 19×12 size diagram is 19 squares wide and 12 squares deep.)

As a rule, you will find that practically every publisher uses his own standard for the width of the acrostic puzzle diagrams appearing in his magazines. The depth of the diagrams may vary slightly; however, the width usually remains the same throughout the publisher's crossword puzzle magazines. For example, if the widths of acrostic puzzle diagrams in one puzzle magazine are 19 squares wide, you will usually find that the widths of the acrostic diagrams will be identical in all the puzzle magazines published by that same publisher.

Of course, there are exceptions to the rule. I found one crossword puzzle magazine that contains acrostic puzzles with three different widths—15, 16, and 19 squares wide.

Whenever you use quotations in acrostic puzzles, make it a rule to use only subject matter that is in the public domain. "Public domain," in this case, refers to literary material that is no longer protected by a copyright.) If you follow this rule, you will avoid any charges of plagiarism for use of literary material without permission.

Of course, you can use material from books, magazines, newspapers, etc. that isn't in the public domain; however you must have the publisher's permission to reproduce the material. Getting this permission requires time; it involves correspondence with the publisher(s). That's why I suggest that you use only material in public domain.

When you select quotations for your acrostics, be sure that the quotations fit into the diagrams for which they are selected.

Avoid quotations that aren't complete thoughts. Note the following example. It is an excellent example of a quotation that isn't a complete thought.

> Mary had a little lamb,
> Its fleece was white as snow;
> And everywhere that Mary went,

In the selection of quotations, make it a rule to select material from the works of authors whose names aren't too long. Also select quotations with short or medium length titles—depending, of course, on the lengths of the quotations. If you follow this rule, you should be able to confine your definitions to the 26 letters of the alphabet.

Before you use double-designating letters (for example, AA, BB, etc.) for your definitions, be sure the publisher uses them. Some publishers allow this practice and some do not. I suggest that you be guided by the instructions in the requirement sheets and by the acrostic puzzles in the publisher's crossword puzzle magazines.

If you wish to select a quotation for your acrostic puzzle in which the combination of the author's name and the title of his (or her) work contains too many letters, there are several ways in which you can shorten the combined number of letters in the author's name and title of his work.

In order to avoid using double-designating letters for the definitions, most editors will permit you to shorten or completely eliminate the author's first and/or middle name. As a rule, however, the author's last name and the complete title of his work must be retained. And then, of course, there are some editors who will even permit you to shorten the title if it is too long.

To illustrate the procedure for shortening the author's name, let's take the name of William Shakespeare who wrote the play *Hamlet*.

Ordinarily, the author's name and the title of his work would appear on the quotations page in the following manner:

Author: William Shakespeare
Work: "Hamlet"

If you wish to use only the initial of the author's first name, you can do it as follows:

Author: W(illiam) Shakespeare
Work: "Hamlet"

The parentheses which enclose the letters "illiam" of the first name indicate to the editor that that part of the author's name has been omitted in the puzzle. So, when you lay out the first letters of the answer words for the acrostic puzzle, the letters are layed out as shown:

W SHAKESPEARE

By using only the initial of the author's first name, six definitions and six answer words have been eliminated from the puzzle.

To illustrate further how an author's long name can be shortened, study the following examples:

#1:
Author:　John G(reenleaf) Whittier

#2:
Author:　J(ohn) G(reenleaf) Whittier

#3:
Author:　(John) (Greenleaf) Whittier

#4:
Author:　J G Whittier

About the only important point to remember when you wish to shorten an author's name for use in an acrostic puzzle is that you must enclose in parentheses that part of the name which you wish to eliminate from the puzzle.

Some editors break the rule and permit puzzle constructors to shorten titles. Whenever this practice is permitted, you will find that the full title of the author's work is given; however, that part of the title which is to be eliminated from the puzzle is enclosed in parentheses.

One of the outstanding differences between the acrostic and the regular crossword puzzle is in the way that the definitions and the answer words are presented on the definition page(s). For example, in the regular crossword puzzle, the definitions are designated by numbers, as shown in the following example.

1.　Ardent affection　LOVE

In the acrostic puzzle, the definition numbers are replaced by designating letters, as shown in the following example.

A. Ardent affection　$\underset{21}{\text{L}}$　$\underset{7}{\text{O}}$　$\underset{3}{\text{V}}$　$\underset{10}{\text{E}}$

(Some publishers use a period after each designating letter, as shown in the preceding example, and some publishers do not. So be guided by the instructions in the requirement sheet or by the publisher's style.)

And keep in mind the fact that the letters and the numbers in the diagram sections of the puzzles must be checked carefully to be sure that they correspond with the letters and the numbers in the answer words.

Some publishers allow two or more words to be used in the answers for single definitions, as shown in the following example.

B. Away from residence $\overline{\text{N}}\ \overline{\text{O}}\ \overline{\text{T}}\ \ \overline{\text{A}}\overline{\text{T}}\ \ \overline{\text{H}}\ \overline{\text{O}}\ \overline{\text{M}}\ \overline{\text{E}}$
$\phantom{\text{Away from residence }}\ \ 3\ \ 10\ \ 17\ \ \ 2\ \ 8\ \ \ 21\ \ 19\ \ 11\ \ 18$

I suggest that you avoid this. Acrostic puzzles are very difficult to solve even when only single words are used for the answers. So why make them even more difficult to solve by using multiple words for the answers?

The acrostic puzzle, when fully completed, consists of three parts —the quotation page, the diagram page, and the definition page(s).

The quotation page contains the puzzle constructor's name and address, the author's name, the title of his (or her) work, the quotation, the publisher's name, and the number of the page from which the quotation was taken, as shown in Figure 64.

The diagram page contains the puzzle constructor's name and address and the complete diagram with all the letters and the numbers typed in, as shown in Figure 65. (The code number of the puzzle is optional.)

The definition page(s) contain the puzzle constructor's name and address, the designating letters of the definitions, the definitions, the answer words, and the numbers for the letters in the answers, as shown in Figure 66.

Acrostics, like all other types of word puzzles, are constructed in two stages—the rough stage and the finished stage.

In the acrostic puzzle, as opposed to the regular crossword puzzle, the puzzle constructor has many more items to keep track of at one time. So if everything seems to be a bit complicated at first, don't become discouraged. Just read this chapter several times until you thoroughly understand the basic construction.

In this chapter, I'm going to explain in full detail (step by step)

John Doe, Jr.
1635 Woodland Rd.
Cannon, Va. 11776

Author: Vera D. Aniels
Work: False Economy

QUOTATION:

> Even though small cars are cheaper,
> I still went into debt much deeper.
> Ever since my family grew,
> I was forced to purchase two.

The Title Publishing Co.
Quotation taken from page 92.

Figure 64

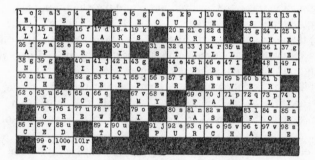

Figure 65

the method I use and find most satisfactory for constructing acrostic puzzles. This method works quite well for me and I'm sure that it will work as well for you.

Before I actually start to construct any acrostic for a specific publication, I study the publisher's requirement sheet for acrostic puzzles. In addition to the instructions in the requirement sheet, I also study the acrostic puzzles in the puzzle magazines of the pub-

John Doe, Jr.
1635 Woodland Rd.
Cannon, Va. 11776

DEFINITIONS   WORDS

A. Steam

$\underset{2}{V}\ \underset{13}{A}\ \underset{27}{P}\ \underset{7}{O}\ \underset{18}{R}$

B. Each without
   exception

$\underset{25}{E}\ \underset{59}{V}\ \underset{60}{E}\ \underset{61}{R}\ \underset{74}{Y}$

C. Make reference to

$\underset{21}{R}\ \underset{1}{E}\ \underset{69}{F}\ \underset{3}{E}\ \underset{29}{R}$

D. Spikelike cluster

$\underset{17}{A}\ \underset{12}{M}\ \underset{22}{E}\ \underset{4}{N}\ \underset{32}{T}$

E. First appearance

$\underset{44}{D}\ \underset{28}{E}\ \underset{46}{B}\ \underset{92}{U}\ \underset{5}{T}$

F. Part of a circle

$\underset{26}{A}\ \underset{57}{R}\ \underset{16}{C}$

G. Scored

$\underset{38}{N}\ \underset{43}{O}\ \underset{39}{T}\ \underset{23}{C}\ \underset{6}{H}\ \underset{37}{E}\ \underset{52}{D}$

H. Article

$\underset{30}{I}\ \underset{42}{T}\ \underset{45}{E}\ \underset{48}{M}$

I. Formerly

$\underset{53}{E}\ \underset{76}{R}\ \underset{11}{S}\ \underset{47}{T}$

J. Drinking, as a cat

$\underset{14}{L}\ \underset{70}{A}\ \underset{55}{P}\ \underset{91}{P}\ \underset{33}{I}\ \underset{41}{N}\ \underset{9}{G}$

K. Close

$\underset{19}{S}\ \underset{24}{H}\ \underset{8}{U}\ \underset{89}{T}$

L. Small number

$\underset{83}{F}\ \underset{54}{E}\ \underset{36}{W}$

M. Largest continent

$\underset{20}{A}\ \underset{31}{S}\ \underset{40}{I}\ \underset{81}{A}$

N. Staggering movement

$\underset{15}{L}\ \underset{49}{U}\ \underset{85}{R}\ \underset{50}{C}\ \underset{51}{H}$

O. Slender flexible whip

$\underset{62}{S}\ \underset{100}{W}\ \underset{79}{I}\ \underset{99}{T}\ \underset{94}{C}\ \underset{10}{H}$

P. Shade tree

$\underset{56}{E}\ \underset{73}{L}\ \underset{71}{M}$

Q. Man's name

$\underset{66}{E}\ \underset{93}{R}\ \underset{72}{I}\ \underset{65}{C}$

R. Monk's hood

$\underset{86}{C}\ \underset{101}{O}\ \underset{78}{W}\ \underset{34}{L}$

S. Be indebted to

$\underset{84}{O}\ \underset{80}{W}\ \underset{98}{E}$

T. Old horse

$\underset{64}{N}\ \underset{96}{A}\ \underset{75}{G}$

U. Lubricated

$\underset{90}{O}\ \underset{63}{I}\ \underset{35}{L}\ \underset{77}{E}\ \underset{88}{D}$

V. Cause to engage

$\underset{67}{M}\ \underset{87}{E}\ \underset{97}{S}\ \underset{95}{H}$

W. Affirmative reply

$\underset{68}{Y}\ \underset{58}{E}\ \underset{82}{S}$

Figure 66

lisher. For example, I check to see whether the publisher uses small or large diagrams for acrostic puzzles. I check to see whether the quotations that are used in these puzzles are written in verse or in prose. I also check to see whether the quotations are of a serious or a humorous nature. Furthermore, I study the magazines' formats for style and other points of interest that may be of help to me.

I find, for example, that the publisher to whom I intend to submit my acrostic puzzles uses short humorous quotations. I also find that all the diagrams for acrostics used by this publication are 15 squares wide. However, the depths of the diagrams vary from 8 to 12 squares.

And now that I have acquired all the necessary information I need in reference to the acrostic puzzle, I am ready to begin constructing the puzzle.

For this particular puzzle, I have selected a short humorous poem that contains 101 letters and 23 spaces between the words. (Incidentally, the spaces between the words of the quotation are designated by the black squares in the diagram.) Since my selected quotation contains a total of 124 letters and spaces, I find that this particular quotation will fit nicely into a diagram that is 15 squares wide and 9 squares deep.

Next, I count the number of letters in the author's name and the title of her work, and I find that they add up to a combined total of 23 letters. Therefore, this means that I will not have to use double-designating letters (AA, BB, CC, etc.) for my definitions.

At this point, before I proceed any further with the puzzle, I make absolutely sure that all the letters in the author's name and all the letters in the title of the work are found within the quotation. For example, if the author's name or the title of the work contains any letters of the alphabet that don't appear in the quotation, then the quotation can't be used for an acrostic puzzle. Or, if the author's name and the title of the work contain more letters of one character than there are in the quotation, then the quotation can't be used either. If, for example, the author's name and the title of the work contain three V's, the quotation can't be used for the puzzle, because this particular quotation contains only two V's—e*v*en and e*v*er. All of this information must be known before I can proceed with the puzzle. Otherwise, I may spend a great deal of time working on the puzzle only to eventually discover that I can't use the quotation. However, when I'm absolutely sure that I can use the quotation, I proceed to work on the rough stage of my acrostic puzzle in the following manner:

1. On a separate sheet of paper, I roughly print the author's name, the title of the work, and the quotation. Beneath the quotation, I print the publisher's name and the page number from which the quotation has been taken. And since this quotation has been taken from a book that is in public domain, no permission is required from the publisher to reproduce this particular poem. (Actually, this quotation is an original poem which was composed primarily as an illustration for this particular chapter; therefore, I need no permission to use it in my puzzle. However since I'm giving an actual example of the procedure that I follow in constructing an acrostic puzzle, I refer to this particular poem just as though it were really taken from a book.)

2. I draw a 10×11 size diagram on fairly heavy cardboard. Each square in the diagram is approximately ⅝″ square. (The size of the squares really isn't that important; however, I like to work with large letters, so I make the squares in my diagram larger than necessary. In this way I can spot mistakes in the spelling much easier.)

3. I print the quotation in the diagram—one letter to each square. (These letters are printed with ink, and they are fairly large in size.)

4. I take a pair of scissors and cut the diagram into individual squares—one letter to each square.

5. In this step, I separate the letters of the quotation into individual groups. For example, all the A letters go into one group, all the B letters into the second group, all the C letters into the third group, etc.

6. When all the individual letters of one character have been separated into individual groups, I pick out 23 letters that spell out the author's name and the title of her work—VERA D ANIELS FALSE ECONOMY.

(If by any chance you own the word game "Scrabble," you can use the letters that come with this game to lay out the quotations. The letters in "Scrabble" are printed in large characters on heavy cardboard, which is ideal for constructing acrostic puzzles.)

7. I lay the 23 letters (VERA D ANIELS FALSE ECONOMY) in a vertical line so that when they are read from top to bottom they will spell out the author's name and the title of her work, as shown in the first column of letters in Figure 66. (This particular step is an important one, because the whole acrostic puzzle develops gradually around this step.)

8. With the remaining letters of the cut up quotation, I proceed to form 23 complete words. Each one of the words must start with one of the letters that are used to spell out the author's name and the title of her work. For example, the first word must start with the letter V which I have layed out at the top of the first column of letters. The second word must start with the letter E, the third word with the letter R, etc., until all the remaining 78 letters of the quotation have been used to form 23 complete words.

(The important thing that must be remembered in this particular step is that the letters that spell out the author's name and the title of the author's work can't be moved around or changed in any manner. These letters must remain stationary. However, the remaining letters of the quotation can be moved around and changed, as often as necessary, from one word to another until all the letters of the quotation have been used to form as many words as are necessary for the acrostic puzzle.)

9. After the 23 words have been completely formed, I count the number of letters in the words to be absolutely sure that I have used all of the 101 letters in the quotation. If, for example, I use more than 101 letters or less than 101 letters to form the 23 answer words, the acrostic puzzle will be worthless. I must use only the 101 letters that are found in the quotation—not one letter less and not one letter more.

10. When the total number of letters (101) that form the 23 answer words check out correctly, I print the 23 answer words on two clean sheets of paper. Actually these two sheets of paper become my first set of rough definition pages.

(Incidentally, I don't use any proof sheets for acrostic puzzles, because I can easily keep track of all the answer words in the puzzle. There really isn't any problem of using duplicate words in the answers.)

11. I print the definitions for the 23 answer words.

12. After each definition I print a designating letter for each definition.

13. In this particular step, I prepare my second set of rough definition pages simply by reversing the order of the words, the definitions, and the designating letters for the definitions. When this step is completed, I lay the two rough definition pages aside for the time being.

13. I draw a 15×9 square rough diagram for my acrostic puzzle.

This diagram is drawn in the following manner:

I take one of my large mimeographed 17×22 diagrams (which takes up the entire page and is made up of ½" squares) and mark off a 15×9 square section and in a matter of a minute I have a rough diagram for my acrostic puzzle.

(If you need just a few rough diagrams to practice on, I suggest that you draw them by hand. And then, if you decide that you would like to continue constructing acrostic puzzles—and I doubt very much that you will—you can have a hundred or so large-size diagrams mimeographed for your own use. The reason that I use ½" squares in my rough diagrams for acrostic puzzles is that when I print the letters of the quotation, the designating letters of the definitions, and the numbers in the individual squares of the diagrams, I don't have to crowd them one on top of the other. I like a fairly large amount of space in the individual squares of the rough diagrams, especially in the diagrams for acrostic puzzles.)

14. In the marked off section of the rough diagram, I print the quotation for my acrostic puzzle. (Between each word of the quotation, I leave a blank square which is inked in solid after the quotation is completed. Actually, these black squares separate the individual words in the diagram.)

15. I number (in rotation) each square in the diagram that contains a letter of the quotation—starting with the number 1 in the first square and ending with the number 101 in the last square, as shown in Figure 67. Then, from this point on, I work on the rough diagram page and the rough definition pages at the same time.

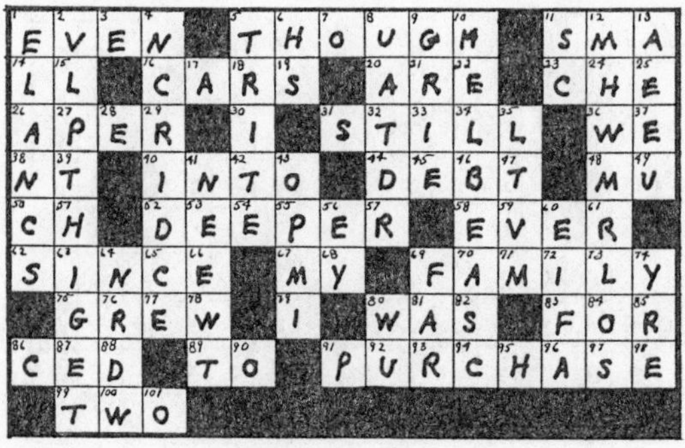

Figure 67

16. At this stage of the puzzle, I take the number that appears in each individual square in the rough diagram and transfer it to the appropriate letter in one of the answer words that appear on the rough definition pages. Then I take the designating letter of each definition and transfer it to the proper square in the rough diagram.

For example, I will start with the first answer word, VAPOR.

First, I must select five letters in the rough diagram that will spell out the word VAPOR.

Next, I must transfer the five square numbers of these five selected letters in the rough diagram and place the numbers beneath the five letters which spell out the word VAPOR on the rough definition page.

Finally, I must take the designating letter (A) of the first definition and transfer it to the five squares (in the rough diagram) that contain the five letters spelling VAPOR.

These steps are accomplished in the following manner:

(a) Looking at the quotation in the rough diagram (Figure 67), I find that the number 2 square in the diagram contains the letter V which also happens to be the first letter in the answer word VAPOR. So I transfer the number 2 to the rough definition page and place it beneath the letter V in the word VAPOR.

(b) The first definition (Steam) for the first answer word (VAPOR) is designated by the letter A. So I transfer the letter A of the first definition to the rough diagram and place it in the upper right-hand corner of the square that contains the letter V and the number 2, as shown in Figure 68.

(c) Looking at the quotation in the diagram (Figure 68), I find

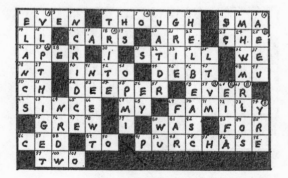

Figure 68

that the square number 13 contains the letter A, which also happens to be the second letter in the word VAPOR. So I transfer the number 13 to the rough definition page and place it beneath the letter A in the word VAPOR. Then, I transfer the designating letter (A) of the first definition to the rough diagram and place it in the upper right-hand corner of the square that contains the letter A and the number 13, as shown in Figure 68.

(d) Since the third letter of the word VAPOR is the letter P, I select the square number 27 in the diagram which contains the letter P. So I transfer the number 27 to the rough definition page and place it beneath the letter P in the word VAPOR, as shown in Figure 66. And since I am still working on the first answer word, I transfer the designating letter (A) of the first definition to the rough diagram and place it in the upper right-hand corner of the square that contains the letter P and the number 27, as shown in Figure 68.

(e) Next, I select the square number 7 in the diagram that contains the letter O. So I transfer the number 7 to the rough definition page and place it beneath the letter O in the word VAPOR, as shown in Figure 66. And since I'm still working on the first answer word, I transfer the designating letter (A) of the first definition to the rough diagram and place it in the upper right-hand corner of the square that contains the letter O and the number 7, as shown in Figure 68.

(f) Now I select the square number 18 in the diagram that contains the letter R. So I transfer the number 18 to the rough definition page and place it beneath the letter R in the word VAPOR. And since the letter R still belongs to the first answer word, I transfer the designating letter (A) of the first definition to the rough diagram and place it in the upper right-hand corner of the square that contains the letter R and the number 18, as shown in Figure 68.

(g) I select the squares numbered 25, 59, 60, 61, and 74. The letters in these five squares spell out the second answer word, EVERY. So I transfer these five numbers (25, 59, 60, 61, and 74) from the five squares in the rough diagram to the rough definition page and place them beneath the letters of the word EVERY, as shown in Figure 66. And since the second definition, which defines the word EVERY, is designated by the letter B, I transfer the letter B to the rough diagram and place it in the upper right-hand corner of the squares that contain the letters E, V, E, R, and Y and the numbers 25, 59, 60, 61, and 74, as shown in Figure 68.

The numbers for the remaining 21 answer words are transferred from the rough diagram to the rough definition pages in exactly the same manner as shown in steps a, b, c, d, e, f, and g. The designating letters for the remaining definitions are also transferred from the rough definition pages to the rough diagram and placed in the proper squares in the same manner as shown in steps a, b, c, d, e, f, and g.

17. As a final step in the rough stage of the acrostic puzzle, I check the numbers beneath the letters of the answer words on the rough definition pages with the numbers in the squares of the rough diagram to be sure that they correspond with one another. At the same time I check the designating letters of the definitions to be sure that they are placed in the proper squares in the rough diagram.

Please note that there is no set rule to follow for selecting the square numbers in the diagram. You don't have to select the square numbers in rotation; you can select the square numbers from any part of the diagram.

Before I start to explain the procedure that I follow in constructing the finished stage of the acrostic puzzle, I would like to point out that transferring the numbers from the squares in the rough diagram to the letters of the answer words on the rough definition pages and then transferring the designating letters of the definitions to the proper squares in the rough diagram is really the simple part of the acrostic puzzle construction. You will find it's practically impossible to use duplicate numbers or duplicate definition letters in the same puzzle. A mere glance at the diagram will show you which numbers in the diagram squares have been already used for the answer words. For example, any square in the rough diagram that contains a designating letter of a specific definition is an indication that the number of that particular square in the rough diagram has already been transferred to a specific letter in one of the answer words on the rough definition pages.

For the finished stage of the acrostic puzzle, I proceed with the quotation page first, the diagram page next, and the definition pages last. The finished stage of the acrostic puzzle is completed in the following manner:

18. To prepare the quotation page, I take a clean sheet of paper and insert it in the typewriter. In the upper right-hand corner of the page (four spaces down from the top), I print my name and address.

19. About one third down from the top of the quotation page, I type the author's name and the title of the author's work.

20. Four spaces below the title of the author's work, I type the quotation.

21. Four spaces below the quotation, I type the publisher's name and the page number from which the quotation has been taken. This step completes the quotation page. (The spacing on the quotation page is made according to my own set of rules. However, double spacing between the lines of the quotation is a must.)

22. To prepare the diagram page, I take a clean sheet of paper and draw a 15×9 square diagram—15 squares wide and 9 squares deep.

(With one exception, the procedure I follow for drawing acrostic puzzle diagrams is practically the same as the procedure I follow for drawing the diagrams for the regular crossword puzzles.)

When I outline an acrostic puzzle diagram with dots, I allow four spaces between all the horizontal dots in the outline—one space more than I allow between the horizontal dots in the outline for the regular crossword puzzle diagrams.

The squares in the diagrams for acrostic puzzles must be wide enough to accommodate three numbers and one letter in each individual square.

I never use double-designating letters for any of my definitions; however, if I were to use them, I would allow five spaces between all the horizontal dots in the diagram outlines.

And while I'm still on the subject of diagrams, I would like to point out that I know of no specific rule to follow for placing the acrostic puzzle diagram on the diagram page. I generally draw a sample diagram, cut it out with a pair of scissors, and place it on the diagram page (clean sheet of paper). Then, I move the cut-out diagram around to different positions on the diagram page until I find a position on the diagram page that is pleasing to the eye. Next, holding the cut-out diagram in a fixed position, I draw four dots on the diagram page—one dot at each corner of the cut-out diagram. When the dots are completed, I insert the diagram page into the typewriter and proceed to outline the diagram with dots in the usual manner.

I have found that master diagrams aren't very practical for acrostic puzzles because the diagram sizes for these types of puzzles vary so much from publication to publication and from puzzle to puzzle. However, if acrostic puzzles are being submitted to a specific publisher who uses diagrams of a uniform size for these puzzles, then it would be wise to make up a master diagram.

For the larger size diagrams for acrostic puzzles, I give the diagram page a quarter turn and then draw the diagrams lengthwise on diagram pages, as shown in Figure 69.)

23. I mark off and ink in all the black squares in the diagram.

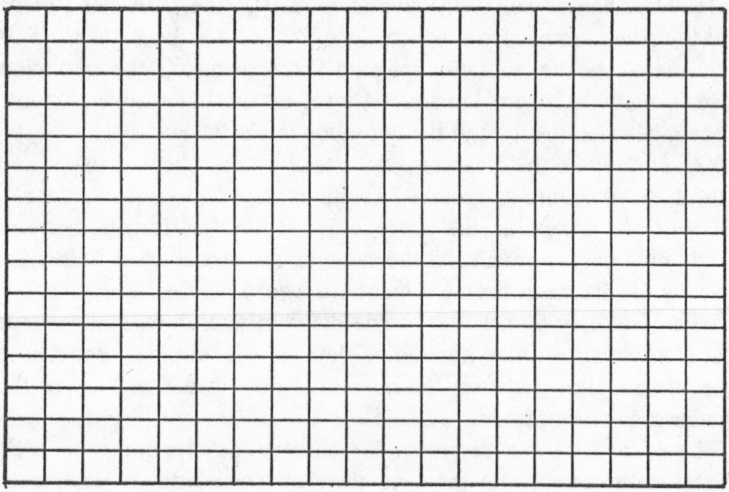

Figure 69

24. I insert the diagram page into the typewriter. In the upper right-hand corner of the diagram page, I type my name and address.

25. I drop down to the diagram and type in all the necessary numbers and all the designating letters of the definitions in the proper squares of the diagram, as shown in Figure 70.

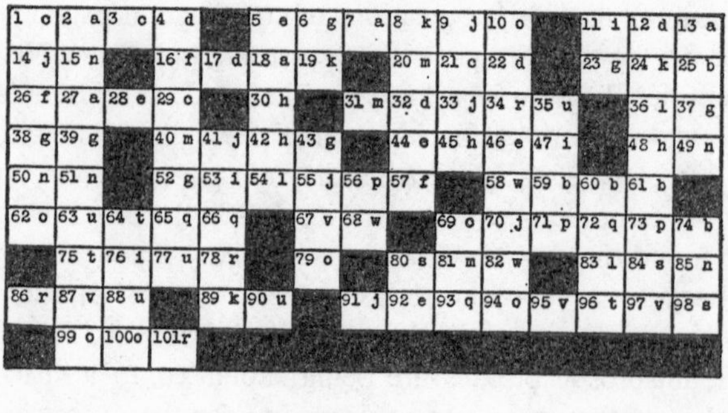

Figure 70

26. I roll the diagram page back to the number 1 square in the diagram. I readjust the diagram page so that the letters of the quotation will be centered in the lower sections of the squares in the

diagram. And then, I proceed to type in the quotation in capital letters.

27. I take the diagram page out of the typewriter, check the spelling of the words in the diagram, and print the code number of my puzzle in the lower right-hand corner of the diagram page. This step completes the diagram page.

28. The definition page for the acrostic puzzle is typed as shown in Figure 66. For this particular type of puzzle, I allow three spaces between the definitions. The lines between the letters of the answer words and the numbers are three spaces long and they are typed three spaces apart.

(Incidentally, if the definitions and the answer words for this type of puzzle are longer than ordinary, the lines between the letters of the answer words and the numbers can be reduced to two spaces, and the spacing between the lines can be reduced to two spaces.)

As an added precaution, I go over all the words in the puzzle to be sure that they are spelled correctly, because misspelled words do manage to get by occasionally on the first check. This step completes the finished stage of the acrostic puzzle.

When I submit acrostic puzzles to the publishers, I always submit them with the diagram page on top, the quotation page in the middle, and the definition pages on the bottom.

This is a rather long explanation, but you must remember that this is a difficult puzzle to construct. To summarize:

1. Study the publisher's requirement sheet for acrostic puzzles.

2. Study the acrostic puzzles in the crossword puzzle magazines of the publishers to whom you intend to submit your puzzles.

3. Check to see what diagram sizes the publisher uses for his acrostic puzzles.

4. Check to see whether the quotations in the acrostic puzzles are written in verse or in prose.

5. Check to see whether the quotations are of a serious or a humorous nature.

6. Select a quotation for your acrostic puzzle.

7. Count the number of letters and the number of spaces in your selected quotation.

8. Print (or write) the author's name and the title of the author's work.

9. Check to see whether every letter in the author's name and in the title of the author's work can be found in the quotation.

10. On a separate sheet of paper, roughly print (or write) the au-

thor's name, the title of the author's work, the quotation, the publisher's name, and the number of the page from which the quotation was taken.

11. Draw a diagram that is large enough to accommodate all the letters in the quotation. Use ⅝″ squares in the diagram.

12. Print the quotation in the diagram—one letter to each square.

13. With a pair of scissors, cut the diagram into individual squares —one letter to each square.

14. Separate all the letters of the quotation into separate groups of characters—A's, B's, C's, etc.

15. Pick out the letters (from the cut-up quotation) that will spell out the author's name and the title of his work.

16. On a table or desk, lay out the letters that spell out the author's name and the title of his work, in a vertical line.

17. With the remaining letters of the quotation, form a word for each letter that is used to spell out the author's name and the title of the work.

18. Count the number of letters in the newly formed words to be sure that you have used all the letters in the quotation.

19. On clean sheets of paper (the ⚹1 rough definition pages), print (or write) in a vertical line all the words you have formed from the cut-up quotation.

20. Print (or write) a definition for each word you have formed from the letters of the quotation.

21. Print (or write) the designating letter after each definition.

22. On clean sheets of paper (the ⚹2 rough definition pages), reverse the order of the words, the definitions, and the designating letters of the definitions on the ⚹1 rough definition pages so that the designating letters of the definitions appear first, the definitions next, and the answer words last.

23. For the rough stage of the acrostic puzzle, draw a rough diagram to fit your quotation.

24. Print your quotation in the rough diagram. (Allow one space between each word in the quotation.)

25. Ink in all the necessary black squares in the rough diagram.

26. Number each square in the rough diagram—that is, number each white square in the diagram.

27. Transfer the numbers from the squares in the rough diagram to the letters of the answer words appearing on the ⚹2 rough definition pages.

28. Transfer the designating letters of the definitions to the proper squares in the rough diagram.

29. Check the numbers and the letters in the rough diagram to be sure that they correspond with the letters and the numbers on the rough definition pages.

30. Type the quotation page—this includes your name, address, author's name, the title of the author's work, the publisher's name, and the number of the page from which the quotation was taken.

31. Draw a diagram on the diagram page.

32. Mark off and ink in all the necessary black squares in the diagram.

33. On the diagram page, type your name and address, the quotation in capital letters (one letter to each square), the numbers of the squares, and the designating letters of the definitions.

34. Type the definition pages—these pages include your name and address, the designating letters of the definition, the definitions, the answer words, and the numbers beneath the letters of the answer words.

35. Check to see whether the numbers, the designation letters of the definitions and the letters of the quotation in the diagram correspond with the numbers, the designating letters of the definitions and the letters of the answer words that appear on the definition pages.

36. Check the puzzle for errors—wrong numbers, wrong designating letters, misspelled words, etc.

X Criteria

All publishers of crossword puzzle magazines have their own standards by which they judge the quality of the crossword puzzles and other types of word puzzles.

In order to be accepted for publication, crossword puzzles, as well as all other types of word puzzles, must meet the publisher's standards—that is, they must conform to the publisher's styles, rules, and special requirements.

Some publishers set their standards rather high so that they are difficult to comply with. However, most publishers of crossword puzzle magazines use standards that aren't too difficult—even for the beginner—to meet.

All good puzzles must contain certain qualities in order to meet the standards set by the publishers of crossword puzzle magazines.

Publishers of puzzle magazines usually purchase crossword puzzles and other types of word puzzles that are—

Easy to solve (easy answer words and definitions).

Accurate (free from error).

Legible (easy to read).

Interesting (interesting definitions and answer words).

Neat (professional looking, without smudges, noticeable erasure marks, dirty fingerprints, etc.

If you can construct crossword puzzles or other types of word puzzles that contain these five qualities, you will have no difficulty in selling them.

Neatness, the last distinctive quality mentioned, is rather an important one and should not be overlooked, because in order to get an editor to look at your puzzles, the puzzles must have something to attract his attention, something that will make an editor take a second look at your puzzles. Your puzzles should have that "Hey! Look at me!" appearance.

In the construction of all puzzles, a certain amount of care must be taken with the diagram pages and the definition pages so that the finished puzzles are attractive.

Of course, you must follow the publisher's instructions and abide by his rules. However, that really isn't enough. There is another factor that contributes to the attractiveness of crossword puzzles—the arrangement of the puzzle. This includes such aspects as uniform diagram and definition pages, uniform margins on all pages, uniform spacing between the lines, the numbers, and the headings. Your name and address should appear at the same point on all the pages. Your diagrams should be placed in the same location on all the diagram pages, and all the definition and answer words should begin at the same point on all the definition pages. This may sound like a big order, but it really isn't.

Sometimes editors may be overstocked with certain types or sizes of puzzles. In cases such as this, I suppose that they really don't pay too much attention to new puzzles arriving at their desks each day—especially ones from new contributors. Sometimes if they are too busy, they may return your puzzles without even looking at them. However, most editors, even busy ones, who see a batch of attractive-looking puzzles aren't likely to pass them up without looking at them. So if you keep your puzzles attractive looking, easy to solve, legible, interesting, and neat, they will be welcomed by most editors of puzzle magazines. That little bit of extra time and extra care that you give them can often mean the difference between the acceptance and the rejection.

REJECTIONS

Rejection slips are the printed slips of paper that inform the crossword puzzle contributor that the editor can't use the submitted puzzles.

All crossword puzzle constructors are familiar with rejection slips; they are really a part of the crossword puzzle constructing game.

Even experienced puzzle constructors occasionally receive these slips in their mail.

Rejections don't necessarily mean that your work lacks merit. In most cases, the puzzles are rejected because the constructor isn't familiar with the publisher's requirements, or because the publisher is overstocked with certain types or sizes of puzzles. Mainly, though, rejections indicate that the constructor—especially the beginner—is unfamiliar with the publisher's requirements.

If crossword puzzles (or other types of word puzzles) are rejected by one publisher, don't become discouraged. Check the needs of other publications and submit the rejected puzzles to one of them. You may have to retype the definitions to conform with the publisher's requirements, but that is really a minor problem. Usually crossword puzzles that are constructed to meet the requirements of a certain publication can be reworked to meet the needs of another publication.

Sometimes the editor will enclose a note with the rejection slip informing you that he is overstocked with that particular type or size of puzzle. So if you don't wish to rework your rejected puzzles to meet the requirements of other publications, you can lay your rejected puzzles aside for a few months and then resubmit them to the same publication. However, the important thing to remember about all puzzles is that they should be kept in circulation until they are accepted for publication. Keep sending them out. Let the editors see what you have to offer.

If you submit rejected puzzles to another publication, don't let the editor see that your puzzles have been making the rounds. If they have been handled roughly by a careless staff, freshen them up. Retype the definition pages if you must to make them look newly constructed. If the diagram pages are soiled or look ragged, draw new diagrams. You may even find a few errors that probably caused the rejections in the first place. And remember . . . neatness counts. Puzzles that have a clean professional look stand a much better chance of being accepted by fussy editors.

Some grounds for rejections are:

Too many difficult answer words. (Use easy, common, everyday words.)

Too many difficult, long, or complicated definitions. (Use common definitions that can be understood by everyone.)

Too many missing-word definitions. (Keep them at a minimum.)

Diagrams are not symmetrical. (Keep them square.)

Two identical words, or another form of the same word, in the same diagram. (This is a major problem. Use a proof sheet.)

Words used in the diagram which can't be found in the dictionary. (Use only the words that are found in the dictionary which you name as the source of reference.)

Too many trite words. (Avoid them whenever you possibly can.)

Too many two- or three-letter words in one puzzle. (Keep them at a minimum.)

Too many abbreviations in one puzzle. (Some publishers limit the number of abbreviations that are permitted in one puzzle. So keep them at a minimum.)

Too many black squares in the diagram. (Some publishers limit the number of black squares that are permitted in different puzzle sizes.)

Too many foreign, obsolete, or archaic words in the diagram. (Avoid them whenever you possibly can. Eliminate them entirely from the easy puzzles.)

Morbid or unpleasant words used in the puzzle. (They are taboo in any type of word puzzle.)

Answer words that are only one half of a hyphenated word. (Use no hyphenated words in the diagram sections of any kinds of word puzzles.)

Misspelled words in the definitions. (Check them for accuracy before and after you type them up.)

Misspelled words in the diagram. (This error will always bring a rejection slip.)

And, of course, disregarding any part of the publisher's rules or instructions can also be grounds for rejections.

There are some editors who are kind enough to take the time to write a short note and give you the reason for rejecting your puzzles. In fact, a few of them may even take the time to tell you how you can improve the quality of your puzzles.

Some publishers use printed rejection slips that include a large variety of reasons for the rejections. Whenever these types of rejection slips are used, the editors merely check off the reason(s) for their rejections of your puzzles. This is a very good idea. At least the contributors know the reasons for the rejections. However, most publishers use rejection slips that give no reason or explanation. The publishers just keep the contributors wondering and guessing.

When you have been successful in selling puzzles only once to a certain publication, you have established a kind of a toehold; now the editor feels that he knows you. Play it cool. Don't flood the editor's desk with your puzzles. Take it easy until you have established a foothold. Once you become firmly established with a certain publication, you can gradually increase the number of puzzles you submit every month. In fact, if you are really good, the editor may even ask you to contribute more puzzles for his consideration. He (or she) may even ask you to become a regular contributor.

It isn't unusual for some regular puzzle constructors to contribute twenty or thirty puzzles each month to a publication. Usually regular constructors contribute a given quota of puzzles each month.

So get those puzzles started and get them in circulation. Let the editors know what you can do, and before you know it you will become a professional crossword puzzle constructor and have many of your puzzles published in a variety of magazines. When this happens, you can be sure of a steady flow of checks each month.

Before you get carried away with visions of great wealth, let me assure you that you will not get rich constructing crossword puzzles. However, if you want to earn extra money for some of those little luxuries you would like to have, crossword puzzle constructing is a good way to earn that extra money.

Occasionally, there may be times when you may request requirement sheets for certain kinds of puzzles—and never get them. Some publishers may get overstocked with certain types or sizes of puzzles, and since they don't wish to be bothered with extra puzzles that they will have to return to the contributor, they simply don't answer requests for requirement sheets until their stock of puzzles is depleted and new ones are needed. So if you don't receive the requirement sheet(s) you have requested, wait a month or two and try again.

And then, of course, there are some publishers who will not send out any kind of requirement sheets to new puzzle constructors because they have regular contributors who supply them with all the puzzles they need. Sometimes you may be informed by the editor that he has regular contributors who supply all the puzzles the publication can use. Which, of course, is just a polite way of saying that they don't want to be bothered with your puzzles.

My personal opinion, however, is that most editors, even those who use regular contributors, will look at unsolicited puzzles and even purchase them—particularly if the puzzles are interesting, easy to solve, and meet their requirements.

Even though many editors will not admit it, they all know that there is no guarantee that their regular puzzle contributors will stay with them forever. Puzzle contributors get tired of constructing puzzles and give them up; others find more profitable hobbies. So you see, if publishers wish to stay in business, they do need new puzzle contributors to supply them with all the puzzles they need. No publisher or editor is going to pass up the chance of acquiring a new puzzle contributor who is dependable and qualified to construct the kinds of puzzles that meet the editor's requirements and keep the publisher in business.

I must admit, however, that the beginner does have a problem trying to convince an editor that he is dependable and qualified to construct word puzzles—particularly when there are no requirement sheets available and the beginner has no way of knowing the editor's requirements. On one occasion I had such a problem. Let me tell you how I solved it.

I had sent three requests for requirement sheets for crossword puzzles to a certain editor, but had never received a reply. In fact, even my stamped, self-addressed envelopes had never been returned to me. I felt, however, that if I could only get the editor to look at my puzzles, I could sell them to her. (The reason that I was so confident was that just a few days before, another editor had written me to the effect that I did good work and she would like to have me as a regular contributor. And, of course, I accepted her generous offer gladly.)

So instead of writing for a requirement sheet again, I decided that I would send the editor a few samples of my puzzles so that she could see my work, and then, perhaps I could convince her that I had the ability to construct crossword puzzles that were comparable in quality to the puzzles she published.

First, I studied the crossword puzzles in her magazine until I was thoroughly familiar with the types she preferred. (Incidentally, all the crossword puzzles in the magazine were of one size—15×15 size in the easy and medium classifications.)

Second, I selected three 15×15 size diagram designs that contained the minimum number of two- and three-letter words.

Third, I constructed three 15×15 easy puzzles. Special care was taken with these puzzles. I used only easy answer words and easy definitions in these puzzles—no trite, obsolete, archaic, morbid, foreign, or difficult words were used. The three puzzles were double-checked for accuracy and errors. They were perfect.

Fourth, I sat down and typed a letter to the editor. The wording went something like this:

Dear Miss —:

I am fully aware of the fact that many editors of crossword puzzle magazines have regular crossword puzzle contributors who supply them with all the puzzles that they need each month.

When everything is running smoothly, this is an ideal system for an editor to follow. However, many editors fail to take into consideration the fact that regular crossword puzzle contributors, even dependable ones, may, for a variety of reasons, suddenly stop contributing crossword puzzles without giving the editors advance notice. When this occurs, they must be replaced with other reliable puzzle contributors. If in the near future you find that you have an opening on your list of regular contributors, will you please be so kind as to look at a few of my sample puzzles to see whether they meet your requirements so that I may know if there is any hope for me of ever becoming one of your regular crossword puzzle contributors.

At the present time, I am contributing to two publications with over 350 published puzzles to my credit. However, I still find enough spare time to take on an additional assignment if one should come my way.

I am enclosing three sample copies of my finished work. These three sample copies may not meet all of your requirements, because I do not have your requirement sheet for crossword puzzles. These puzzles were constructed by simply studying the puzzles in your crossword puzzle magazines. However, they will give you a general idea of my ability to construct interesting puzzles and show you the high quality of my workmanship.

If you would like me to construct some samples that meet your requirements, I will be pleased to do so. Just send me your requirement sheet, in addition to the sizes and the types of puzzles that you are in need of at the present time—easy, medium or difficult; any size from 9×9 to 23×23.

Thank you for taking the time to read this letter.

Sincerely yours,

I enclosed the letter with the three sample copies of my puzzles in a 9×12 envelope. I also enclosed a 9×12 stamped, self-addressed envelope, which I folded in two, and mailed it to the editor.

In ten days the puzzles were returned with a note from the editor which said:

Dear Miss Daniels:

We are always interested in original puzzles from new contributors. We cannot use these puzzles since our word count is now limited to 82 words. Please submit some regular 15×15 size crossword puzzles for consideration (preferably easy and medium ones).

Thank you,

So I constructed five 15×15 size easy and medium crossword puzzles in which the word count was limited to 82 words and submitted them to the editor. All the puzzles were accepted for publication. After that, I had no problem selling my puzzles to this particular editor.

This just goes to prove that if you can construct interesting puzzles of a high quality and neat workmanship, and if you have the determination and can convince an editor to look at your puzzles, you can also get the editor to purchase them.

Incidentally, even though I have sold many crossword puzzles to this particular editor, she never did send me a requirement sheet for crossword puzzles. This also goes to prove that it's possible to sell crossword puzzles even though you don't have the magazine's requirement sheet. However, I recommend that you use requirement sheets whenever it's possible. Of course, you can acquire a vast amount of information simply by studying the puzzles in puzzle magazines. However, there is much more information to be found in the requirement sheet. With requirement sheets, there is no guess work. *All* the rules and requirements are printed in black on white so that you can't make any mistakes.

On one other occasion, even though I had the publisher's requirement sheet for crossword puzzles, my submitted puzzles were rejected several times by a certain editor. So one day I sat down and wrote the editor a letter. It was worded something like this:

Dear Sir:

Several times you have rejected, without any explanation, my puzzles that were submitted for your consideration. Since I can't find anything radically wrong with the rejected puzzles, I can only assume that perhaps I am submitting the wrong sizes or the wrong types of puzzles.

In order to save you the trouble of returning my puzzles, and in order to save me the trouble of constructing and submitting puzzles that you can't use, I have compiled a list of puzzles that I am capable of constructing. Will you please check off the sizes and the types of puzzles that you are in need of at the present time. I guarantee that all the puzzles will meet your requirements and will be comparable in quality with the puzzles that are published in your crossword puzzle magazines.

Thank you,

I sent the letter and the compiled list of puzzles to the editor of this particular publication, and in a few days the compiled list of puzzles was returned to me with an order for seven crossword puzzles. (For a sample copy of my list of puzzles, see Figure 70.) Once I knew

Crossword Puzzles

Regular	Easy	Medium	Difficult	Diagram-less
( ) 11x11	( )	( )	( )	( )	"
( ) 13x13	( )	( )	( )	( )	"
( ) 15x15	( )	( )	( )	( )	"
( ) 17x17	( )	( )	( )	( )	"
( ) 19x19	( )	( )	( )	( )	"
( ) 21x21	( )	( )	( )	( )	"
( ) 23x23	( )	( )	( )	( )	"

( ) Topical Crossword Puzzles   (name the sizes)
( ) Make-It-Yourself Crossword Puzzles   (name the sizes)
( ) Progressive Blocks Puzzles   ( ) 15x15
        ( ) 19x19
( ) Fill-In Puzzles
( ) Acrostic Puzzles
( ) Chain Word Puzzles

Figure 70

what the editor needed, it was a simple matter to give him the types and the sizes of puzzles that he could use.

On one other occasion, I used this same approach on another editor. It resulted in the sale of some topical puzzles.

Regardless of how tightly closed some editors may keep their doors, you can always find a way to get your foot in them if you will only use your ingenuity.

If you care to use the method I did to get your foot into a publisher's door, be sure that you study his magazines thoroughly so that when you type the list of puzzles that you are capable of constructing, the names on your list will correspond with the names of the puzzles in the publisher's crossword puzzle magazines. As I have pointed out previously, certain types of puzzles are listed under different names in different crossword puzzle magazines. Therefore, it is possible that you will have to type different lists of puzzles for different publications.

Before I close, I would like to leave you with this bit of advice: don't be in too great a hurry to submit your first puzzles to a publication. Make sure that your first puzzles meet *all* of the publisher's requirements, and make sure that they are perfect in all respects. Remember that if your first batch of puzzles isn't up to par, the chances are that the editor isn't going to pay too much attention to any others you may submit later on. Make sure that your first batch of puzzles "rings the bell" on the first try. If all or part of your first puzzles are purchased on your initial try, you really have it made. However, if they are rejected on your first try, don't become discouraged. Make some new puzzles and try again. If you wish to succeed, you must have determination. Also, remember that rejections are a part of the game.